Family Recipes from Mill Iron Farm

By Carolyn Shohet and Nancy Shohet West

Carolyn Shohet
Nancy Shohet West

A NOTE FROM THE AUTHORS

This collection represents recipes that we've passed around, revised, amended, updated, changed, changed some more, and passed around again. By the very nature of the way that families share recipes, it is not always easy to trace each recipe's origins. Where possible, we've included what information we have about how the recipe came to be in our possession, but we apologize if we have missed out on any opportunities for proper attribution.

CONTENTS

Acknowledgments i

Introductions iii

Appetizers 1

Beverages 13

Breakfast, Brunch & Breads 17

Soups 35

Salads & Side Dishes 43

Beef, Lamb, Pork,
Poultry & Seafood 63

Vegetarian Entrées 79

Sauces & Marinades 95

Cookies & Candy 101

Desserts 115

Index 136

ACKNOWLEDGMENTS

Thanks to family members Lauren Shohet, Sophie Richardson, Phoebe Richardson, Sarah Shohet, Hannah Mikhail, Andrew Mikhail, Tim West, Holly West, and Dick Shohet for contributing their ideas and requests for this recipe collection. Thanks also to Kristine Zards Rencs, a talented artist and photographer, for her magnificent cover design.

Carolyn's Introduction: How This Book is Different

I've written and published two cookbooks prior to this one. "Carolyn's Kitchen" was published in 1989 and represented a collection of the many interesting dishes we'd made over the previous fifteen years in the cooking classes I taught out of my home. "Carolyn's Kitchen Revisited," published in 1998, was, just as the name suggests, a sequel of sorts: many new recipes from the cooking I'd done in the decade since the publication of the first book, plus a reprise of the best-loved recipes from that earlier collection.

When my daughter Nancy suggested we join forces to put together a new cookbook, I resisted the idea at first, remembering the years of work that had gone into developing and testing the recipes that made up those first two volumes. But then Nancy explained that this one would be different. It didn't have to be the same top-drawer gourmet dishes for which my cooking class was locally famous. "Let's just put together the recipes we all love and are always passing around," she suggested.

Nancy had something of a vested interest. My eldest daughter Lauren has made many trips out of the country over the years, and Nancy claims that every time Lauren leaves the U.S. for more than 36 hours, she calls Nancy and asks for our Mud Pie Cake recipe. (Apparently something about international travel gives Lauren the urge to bake. Maybe a symptom of jet lag?) When we shared our idea about a recipe collection with Lauren, unprompted, she said, "Be sure to include Mud Pie Cake."

As I work on this third collection, I find myself thinking not about my cooking class students or anonymous cookbook buyers, as I did the first two times around, but my six grandchildren. These are their favorites as well, dishes they've savored at countless family dinners and holiday gatherings over the years, and I imagine that someday they'll want these same recipes at their fingertips to make for their own children and grandchildren.

So whether you are one of my grandchildren or someone who picked up a copy of this book without knowing any of us, I hope you will find it to be useful and tempting. These are our favorites, and we are delighted to gather them at last into one volume. Enjoy!

Nancy's Introduction: "Ask-Twice Recipes"

My mother has always maintained a simple, if perhaps slightly cynical, rule about sharing recipes. "When someone tastes something you've made and asks for the recipe, they are probably just being polite," she says. "It's considered a compliment. But I don't want to go to the trouble of copying over a recipe unless they really mean it. I wait until they ask a second time – then I believe they really want it and aren't just trying to flatter me."

I interpreted this rule my own way. Whenever my mother serves something wonderful that I haven't had before, I say to her, "May I have the recipe? May I have the recipe? There, I asked twice."

Worth noting in this anecdote is that my mother's rule predates the era of the Internet. Sharing recipes is a lot less trouble now than when she used to transcribe them word by word on little index cards. Emailing a recipe you've already stored as an electronic file is pretty simple even if the asker never plans to make it and was indeed just trying to be polite.

But I still love this rule. And so when I tried to describe to my mother the kind of cookbook I thought we should compile, I fell back on her basic rule: "The recipes for which people have asked twice."

This collection represents just that: recipes we share among our family, recipes our friends and relatives ask us for, recipes we've emailed and photocopied and even, in the days before email, transcribed by hand countless times. And they are our favorites as well – the ones we find ourselves reaching for again and again. We hope they will become your favorites as well.

APPETIZERS

Beet Spread

Carolyn's note: This is a very unusual appetizer (not to mention a very colorful and eye-catching one). People who like beets are pleased to find a new way to use them, and those who think they do not care for beets often discover otherwise when they taste this spread. Our long-time friend Fred gets credit for discovering this recipe, although it's his wife Jocie who does the cooking.

Makes about 2 cups. This is an easy recipe to double.

1 large beet (about 8 ounces)
1 cup canned chick peas, drained
½ cup extra virgin olive oil
¼ cup slivered toasted almonds
4 cloves garlic, minced
2 tablespoons red wine vinegar
Salt and pepper to taste

Steam beet, unpeeled, in a covered sauce pan until tender – about 30 minutes, but pierce with a fork to test. Remove the skin while the beet is still warm and cut into cubes.

Place beet cubes in food processor or blender with chick peas and blend to a purée. Then add olive oil, almonds, garlic, and vinegar, and blend just until combined, leave a little texture. Season with salt and pepper to taste.

Serve on thin crackers or melba toast at room temperature or chilled.

Brie en Croûte

Carolyn's note: When I first started showcasing Brie en Croûte at holiday parties, it was considered a novelty. Now, of course, just about everyone has seen it, but not everyone realizes how easy it is to make. And somehow after all these years, it still has the power to impress a hungry crowd of party-goers...

Serves about 12

1 sheet frozen puff pastry, thawed to room temperature
½ cup preserves (such as apricot, seedless raspberry, or pepper jelly)
1/3 cup dried cranberries
¼ cup sliced almonds, lightly toasted
1-pound wheel of Brie
1 egg
1 tablespoon water

Preheat oven to 400°F. Unfold pastry sheet onto lightly floured surface. Use a rolling pin to roll as thin as you can without tearing holes. Cut off corners to make a circle. Transfer dough to a large baking sheet.

Spread preserves over puff pastry to within 1 inch of pastry edge. Sprinkle cranberries and almonds over preserves. Top with wheel of cheese.

Lightly beat together egg and water; then brush edge of pastry circle with some of the egg mixture. Fold two opposite sides over cheese; then do the same with the two remaining sides.

Press edges to seal. Flip over and place seam-side down on baking sheet. Brush top with remaining egg mixture.

Bake for 15 to 20 minutes. Serve warm with crackers.

Cheddar Balls or Wafers

Nancy's note: Cheesy, buttery, and rich, this classic hors d'oeuvres is a perfect starter for a cocktail party or traditional dinner party. Mom makes them as balls; I prefer the wafer shape.

Makes about 3 dozen

½ cup butter, at room temperature
8 ounces grated Cheddar
1 cup flour
1/8 teaspoon cayenne pepper
1 teaspoon dried mustard
1 teaspoon paprika
¼ teaspoon salt

In a large mixing bowl, cream butter and cheese together. In a separate bowl, sift together dry ingredients and then mix into the butter and cheese.

For balls, chill dough and then scoop into balls; for wafers, form dough into logs by rolling it inside a sheet of waxed paper; chill logs; and then slice.

Preheat oven to 350°F. Bake on cookie sheets lined with parchment paper for 12-14 minutes. Let sit for about 5 minutes. Serve warm.

(After forming into balls or wafers, these can be frozen for later use. If baking them straight from the freezer, add about 5 minutes to baking time.)

Chèvre with Herbs and Olives

Nancy's note: My favorite thing about this recipe is that it is one of the very few dishes that actually works best in warm, humid summer weather, since heat and humidity seem to enhance the blending of the flavors. Make it several hours before serving and let it sit.

Serves about 8

8 ounces Chèvre or other soft goat cheese
½ cup extra virgin olive oil
2 cloves garlic, chopped
½ cup Kalamata olives, chopped
¼ cup sundried tomatoes, chopped
2 teaspoons fresh basil, chopped
½ teaspoon fresh rosemary, chopped
¼ teaspoon hot red pepper flakes
½ teaspoon fresh thyme, chopped

Spread cheese about ½ inch thick on a medium-sized serving plate or in a shallow pie plate. Drizzle the olive oil over the cheese. Scatter all remaining ingredients on top. Let sit at room temperature for several hours before serving. Serve with sliced French bread, pita chips or crackers.

Two Recipes for Roasted Seasoned Nuts

Nancy's note: Roasted, seasoned nuts fall into the category of foods for which we will try any new rendition even though we already have versions we love. It's just fun to keep trying different ways to make them. No matter which recipe you use, they are a very popular appetizer as well as a greatly appreciated gift. For gift-giving, I put them in jars and have my daughter Holly decorate the jars with paint, ribbons and glitter. Following are two of our favorite versions.

I. Candied Curried Pecans

Makes about 3 cups

1½ teaspoons onion powder
1½ teaspoons garlic powder
1¼ teaspoons coarse kosher salt
¾ teaspoon curry powder
¼ teaspoon cayenne pepper
2 tablespoons unsalted butter
2 tablespoons honey
3 cups pecan halves

Preheat oven to 250°F. Line large rimmed baking sheet with foil or parchment paper.

In a small bowl, combine onion powder, garlic powder, 1 teaspoon salt, curry powder, and cayenne pepper. Melt butter and honey with remaining ¼ teaspoon salt in large saucepan over medium heat.

Add pecan halves to saucepan and stir to coat; remove from heat. Add spice mixture and toss to coat pecans evenly. Spread pecans in single layer on prepared baking sheet.

Bake pecans until dry and toasted, about 40 minutes. Cool completely. Separate pecans. Store in an airtight container for up to a week.

II. Spiced Mixed Nuts

Makes about 2 ½ cups (easy to double)

2 ½ cups mixed nuts such as almonds, peanuts, pecans, walnuts
1/3 cup sugar
1 ½ teaspoons chili powder
1 teaspoon kosher salt
½ teaspoon ground cumin
¼ teaspoon garlic powder
Good pinch of cayenne pepper
1 egg white

Preheat oven to 300°F. Line a cookie sheet with foil or parchment paper.

Place the nuts in a large bowl. Add the remaining dry ingredients; then pour in egg white and stir until evenly combined.

Mix well. (Hands work best.) Spread mixture in a single layer on cookie sheet. Bake 40 minutes, stirring occasionally. Then turn off oven but leave nuts in for another hour or so as the oven cools.

Store in an airtight container for up to a week.

Dates Stuffed with Almonds Wrapped in Bacon

Carolyn's note: "Wrapped in bacon" is a sure clue that you are using a recipe that dates back to the days depicted in the TV series "Mad Men." That era was known for its fabulous cocktail parties, and not surprisingly, these vintage appetizers remain ever popular, just as bacon does!

Makes 4 dozen

48 individual dried dates, pitted
48 whole almonds, lightly toasted (either blanched or unblanched)
2 pounds bacon, uncooked

Preheat oven to 400°F.

Poke a whole almond into each date. Wrap each date with a half slice of bacon and close with a toothpick through the bottom third of the date, avoiding the almond.

Place dates on a cookie sheet with sides. Bake for 20 minutes or a bit longer, until bacon is crisp.

Drain well on paper towels before serving.

To make ahead, assemble and then freeze dates (before cooking) in a single layer on cookie sheet for about 1 hour before transferring to a plastic bag. Add 10 or 15 minutes to baking time.

Guacamole

Nancy's note: My kids insisted we include this recipe. I demurred, saying, "Everyone knows how to make guacamole!" "But not as well as Grandma makes it," they argued. (I think this was a subtle hint that my guacamole never turns out as well as my mother's, which is true.) So here it is "the way Grandma makes it"!

Makes about 1 cup

1 very ripe avocado
2 tablespoons fresh lemon juice
1 tablespoon minced onion
1 teaspoon Worcestershire sauce
½ teaspoon salt
1/8 teaspoon cayenne pepper
1 clove garlic, minced
1 tablespoon light mayonnaise

In a small mixing bowl, mash avocado with a fork. Then stir in all remaining ingredients. If possible, let sit for an hour or two for flavors to blend.

Lentil Walnut Paté

Carolyn's note: Many of my best recipes come from my good friend, Jocie. She introduced me to this recipe, calling it "meatless chopped liver." It does look like chopped liver, but in my opinion it tastes much better – and I am not even a vegetarian!

Makes about 2 cups

½ cup brown lentils
1½ cups water
¼ cup extra virgin olive oil
2 large onions, sliced
1 pinch sugar
½ cup walnuts
1 packet or teaspoon of vegetable bouillon
3 hardboiled eggs, cut in thirds
1 teaspoon Worcestershire sauce
Salt and pepper to taste

Place lentils in a medium saucepan and cover with water. Simmer gently over medium heat, covered, for about 15 minutes, until water is absorbed and lentils are soft. Drain off any excess water.

Sauté onions with sugar in 2 tablespoons olive oil until caramelized and dark brown, about 30 minutes. They should be caramelized but not burnt. Put all ingredients except remaining 2 tablespoons olive oil in a food processor or blender. Blend, slowly adding remaining olive oil, until mixture is of spreadable consistency. Chill for several hours before serving with thin crackers or raw vegetables.

Three Delicious Dips

Carolyn's note: Dips may seem "retro" in today's world of salsas, pestos, and tapenades, but they go far at big parties and are a good way to introduce some fresh vegetables to the hors d'oeuvres table. Here are three we particularly like. Serve with pita chips or fresh vegetables.

Each recipe makes about 1 cup.

I. Peanut Dip

1 tablespoon vegetable oil
1 large shallot, chopped
1 tablespoon fresh ginger, minced
2 garlic cloves, minced
1 teaspoon curry powder
1/8 teaspoon dried crushed red pepper
1 cup (or more) vegetable broth
½ cup smooth peanut butter (use the supermarket type, not
    old-fashioned or freshly ground)
4 teaspoons fresh lime juice
1 tablespoon soy sauce
1 teaspoon (packed) brown sugar

Heat oil in a large skillet over medium heat. Add shallot, ginger and garlic; sauté until shallot is tender, about 3 minutes. Add curry powder and crushed red pepper. Stir until aromatic, about 15 seconds.

Add to skillet 1 cup broth, peanut butter, lime juice, soy sauce, and brown sugar; whisk to blend. Simmer until mixture thickens, whisking constantly, about 3 minutes. Season with salt and pepper.
Transfer to bowl and cool, stirring occasionally. Cover and refrigerate at least two hours. Thin dip with more broth if needed. Serve chilled or at room temperature.

II. Cottage Cheese Dip

1 cup whole-milk cottage cheese
2 tablespoons sour cream
1 hardboiled egg, finely chopped
1 tablespoon finely chopped fresh chives
1 tablespoon finely chopped fresh dill (or 1 teaspoon dried dill)
½ teaspoon finely chopped garlic
¼ teaspoon salt
1/8 teaspoon black pepper
1/8 teaspoon ground cumin

Blend all ingredients in a food processor until smooth; then chill, covered.

III. Curry Dip

½ cup sour cream
¼ cup light mayonnaise
3 ounces cream cheese, at room temperature
1 teaspoon fresh lemon juice
1 teaspoon curry powder
½ teaspoon ground cumin
½ teaspoon salt
¼ teaspoon turmeric
1/3 cup celery, chopped
1/3 cup cucumber, chopped
1 scallion, trimmed and chopped

Mix together all ingredients except celery, cucumber, and scallion until smooth; then stir in chopped vegetables.

BEVERAGES

Hot Chocolate

Nancy's note: My kids took the concept of this cookbook seriously – it didn't matter to them how prosaic a recipe might be; they just wanted to be sure that somewhere we had written down how to make certain things exactly the way Grandma makes them. Hot chocolate is yet another example.

Makes 3 servings

1/3 cup unsweetened cocoa
¼ cup sugar
½ cup water
2 cups milk

In a medium saucepan, whisk together cocoa and sugar. Stir in water to make a paste. Continue stirring as you bring mixture to a boil over medium heat. Gradually stir in milk. Heat until very hot but not boiling. Top with whipped cream or marshmallows, if desired.

Mint Iced Tea

Carolyn's note: This tea has been a favorite family recipe for as long as I can remember. I've served and copied the formula for many friends. In the summertime, many people have fresh mint growing in their yards or know someone who would be happy to give theirs away!

Makes ½ gallon

½ cup fresh mint leaves
7 cups water
4 tea bags
½ cup sugar or to taste
¾ cup orange juice
¼ cup lemon juice

In a small bowl, pour about 1 cup boiling water over the mint leaves and let steep for a few minutes.

In another bowl or a large pitcher, pour about 2 cups boiling water over tea bags and sugar; let steep about 5 minutes. Remove tea bags.

Strain mint water and add it to tea. Stir in juices and 4 cups more water. Let cool; serve over ice.

Hot Mulled Cider

Carolyn's note: Hot mulled cider adds ambiance to a cold-weather party merely for the delicious spicy aroma it sends through the house. It is an old-fashioned treat.

Makes 2 quarts

1 medium whole apple, any variety
2 teaspoons whole cloves
1 whole orange, thinly sliced (no need to peel)
½ gallon apple cider
½ cup brown sugar
1 teaspoons ground allspice
Pinch of grated nutmeg
Rum (optional)

Add all ingredients to large soup pot. Simmer until the apple is tender, about 35-40 minutes.

Add 1 or 2 tablespoons rum to each mug before filling with cider. Serve very hot.

BREAKFAST, BRUNCH & BREADS

Brunch Enchiladas

Nancy's note: Inviting guests for brunch can be an easy way to entertain without doing much cooking – just put out muffins, bagels, and fruit. But if you do feel like going to a bit of work for your brunch guests, here's a memorable way to do it.

Serves 8

8 eggs
salt and pepper
2 tablespoons butter
2 small red peppers, diced
3 scallions, sliced
8 large flour tortillas
2 cups grated Monterey Jack
10-ounce can enchilada sauce
½ cup prepared salsa

Avocado Sauce
2 very ripe avocados
¼ cup sour cream
1 tablespoons diced green chilies
1 tablespoon lemon juice
¼ teaspoon Tabasco sauce
¼ teaspoon salt

In a medium mixing bowl, beat eggs with a pinch of salt and a pinch of pepper. Set aside.

In a large skillet, melt butter. Sauté pepper and scallions until soft, about 10 minutes. Add the eggs to the vegetables in the skillet and cook until eggs are softly scrambled.

Preheat oven to 350°F. Spray a 9" x 13" baking pan with nonstick spray. Set one tortilla on a cutting board or other work space. Spoon about 1/3 cup egg mixture into the center of the tortilla. Top it with 1 tablespoon Monterey Jack. Roll the tortilla and place it, seam side down, in the baking dish. Repeat with remaining 7 tortillas.

Mix enchilada sauce and salsa. Spoon over tortillas. Cover pan with foil. Bake for 20 minutes. Remove foil, sprinkle tortillas with remaining Monterey Jack, and bake 10 minutes more.

While enchiladas are baking, mix avocados, sour cream, green chilies, lemon juice, Tabasco, and salt in a blender or Cuisinart. Serve on the side, or top each enchilada with sauce.

Cheese, Egg and Ham Strata

Carolyn's note: This is one of my favorite brunch dishes to make because it must be prepared ahead of time. The mixture should chill for at least 3 hours before baking for 1 hour, so start it several hours ahead or even the night before you plan to serve it.

Serves 6-8

2 tablespoons butter
2 cups of fresh vegetables in bite-sized pieces, such as spinach,
    mushrooms, tomatoes, peppers, etc.
4 cups leftover bread, any kind (rye or pumpernickel work well)
2 cups sharp grated cheese, whatever kinds you have on hand
1 pound cooked ham, cubed, or cooked bacon, chopped (optional)
4 eggs
2 ½ cups milk
2 tablespoons Dijon mustard (or 2 teaspoons dry mustard)
1 teaspoon Worcestershire sauce
½ teaspoon salt
1/8 teaspoon each paprika, black pepper

In a medium skillet, melt butter and sauté vegetables until soft, about 10 minutes.

In a 9" x 9" baking dish sprayed with nonstick spray, scatter about 1/3 of the bread, 1/3 of the sautéed vegetables, 1/3 of the cheese, then 1/3 of the ham. Repeat twice more.

Mix eggs, milk, mustard and seasonings in blender or with whisk. Pour over the layers. Chill at least 3 hours or overnight.

Bake uncovered at 350°F for 1 hour.

Crustless Quiche with Onions and Gruyère

Nancy's note: This recipe and the one following are both ideal for brunch guests on a gluten-free diet. Cheddar rather than Gruyere can be used.

Serves 6-8

2 medium Yukon Gold potatoes, peeled and cut into cubes
2 tablespoons butter
2 medium Spanish onions, chopped
4 eggs
1 ¼ cups heavy cream
1/3 teaspoon ground nutmeg
Salt and pepper
1 cup grated Gruyère

Preheat oven to 350°F. Butter deep 9" or 10" pie plate or baking dish.

Place potato cubes into a medium saucepan and cover with water. Cook until tender, about 20 minutes. Drain. Place in baking dish.

In a large skillet, melt butter. Add onions and sauté until soft, about 15 minutes. Scatter over potatoes in baking dish.

In a medium mixing bowl, beat together eggs, cream, nutmeg, and a pinch each of salt and pepper. Pour egg mixture over potatoes. Sprinkle with Gruyère.

Bake about 45 minutes, or until just set. Wait about 3 minutes before slicing into wedges or squares. Serve warm.

Smoked Salmon and Caramelized Onion Omelet

Nancy's note: This is another good choice for gluten-free guests: smoked salmon dressed up in a flavorful omelet rather than atop a bagel.

Serves 2

4 eggs
Salt and freshly ground pepper to taste
1 tablespoon extra virgin olive oil
1 large white onion, chopped
1 tablespoon butter
2 ounces smoked salmon, finely diced
2 tablespoons sour cream
Minced fresh chives for garnish

In a medium bowl, beat the eggs with the salt and pepper just until blended.

In a medium skillet over medium heat, heat the oil and sauté the onion, stirring frequently, until soft and caramelized, about 20 minutes. Turn onions out of the skillet.

In the same skillet, melt the butter over medium heat. Pour the eggs into the pan and cook, lifting from the edge to let the runny portion flow underneath. When almost set, scatter the caramelized onion and salmon over.

Fold the omelet in thirds. Divide it in half and slide each half onto a plate. Top with sour cream and chives and serve immediately.

Red Pepper and Red Onion Frittata

Carolyn's note: This dish is perfect for a small brunch. It can be served warm or at room temperature, so you can prepare it before guests arrive.

Serves 4-6

3 tablespoons extra virgin olive oil
1 garlic clove, minced
1/3 cup sourdough bread cubes
1 red onion, diced
2 red bell peppers, seeded, de-ribbed and diced
6 eggs
2 tablespoons minced fresh flat-leaf parsley
3 tablespoons minced fresh basil, plus basil sprigs for garnish
Salt and freshly ground pepper to taste
½ cup shredded Fontina

Preheat the oven to 350°F. Grease a 10-inch round baking dish.

In a large skillet over medium heat, heat 1 tablespoon olive oil, add the garlic and bread cubes, and shake the pan until the bread is thoroughly coated and lightly toasted, about 2 minutes. Turn the bread out of the pan.

Heat the remaining 2 tablespoons oil over medium heat and sauté the onion and peppers until soft, about 10 minutes; let cool slightly.

In a medium bowl, beat the eggs just until blended and mix in the parsley, basil, salt, pepper and sautéed vegetables. Pour into the prepared baking dish and sprinkle with the croutons and cheese.

Bake 20 minutes, or until set. Garnish with basil sprigs.

Slow-Cooked Oatmeal with Fruit and Nuts

Carolyn's note: My cousin Marjie Ettlinger, of Highland Park, Illinois, sent me her favorite breakfast recipe. Start it in the crock pot before you go to bed; when you wake up, you'll feel like someone else made you a hot breakfast!

Serves about 8

2 cups steel-cut oats
2 cups diced apples
1 cup dried cranberries
½ cup slivered almonds
½ cup chopped pecans
3 cups water
1 cup milk
1 tablespoon ground cinnamon
1 teaspoon pumpkin pie spice or ¼ teaspoon each ground ginger,
    nutmeg, allspice, and cloves
1 tablespoon butter

Combine all ingredients in a slow cooker or crock pot. Cook on low for 8 hours.

Who's On First Banana Bread

Nancy's note: For a couple of summers, Tim and Holly baked and sold homemade banana bread at our local Farmers' Market. They gained a devoted following! This was their super-successful recipe. My nephew, Andrew, likes his banana bread studded with chocolate chips. So when I'm making it for him, I add 1 cup mini chocolate chips.

Makes 1 large loaf or 3 mini-loaves

Preheat oven to 350°F. Grease one 9" x 5" loaf pan or three mini loaf pans.

3 large or 4 medium-sized slightly overripe bananas
1 cup sugar
1 ½ cups flour
1 ½ teaspoons baking soda
¼ teaspoon salt
¼ cup butter, melted
2 eggs, slightly beaten
½ cup walnuts, chopped (optional)

In an electric mixer, beat bananas and sugar until very well combined.

In a separate medium mixing bowl, combine flour, baking soda, and salt. Add dry ingredients to banana puree and mix by hand or at slow speed with mixer just until combined. Stir in melted butter and eggs (and walnuts if using).

Pour batter into loaf pan(s). Bake about 45 minutes for large loaf or about 35 minutes for small loaves. Let cool about 5 minutes; then unmold onto a cookie rack to cool.

Cream Biscuits

Nancy's note: This recipe comes from Cook's Illustrated. It makes a rich, flaky, delicious biscuit, and it takes less effort than recipes that use butter rather than cream.

Makes 10-12 biscuits

2 cups flour
2 teaspoons sugar
1 teaspoon baking powder
½ teaspoon salt
1½ cups heavy cream

Preheat oven to 425°F. Line a cookie sheet with parchment paper.

In food processor or by hand, mix together dry ingredients. Then blend in cream. When dough is smooth, drop by medium-sized spoonfuls onto prepared cookie sheet.

Bake 15 minutes, until just beginning to brown.

Cheesy Onion Cornbread

Nancy's note: This is a hearty casserole-type bread that everyone seems to like. It goes well with soup and salad. A single recipe is the right size for a family of four with lunchbox leftovers the next day.

Serves 4-6

2 tablespoons butter
1 large onion, very thinly sliced
1 8 ½-ounce package corn muffin mix
1/3 cup milk
1 egg
1 small (8 ounces or so) can cream-style corn
Dash of hot sauce
1 cup sour cream
½ teaspoon salt
¼ teaspoon pepper
1 cup grated Monterey Jack

Preheat oven to 425°F. Grease a square 8- or 9-inch baking pan. Melt butter in a medium skillet. Sauté onion in melted butter over medium heat until lightly browned (about 15 minutes). Set aside to cool.

In a medium mixing bowl, mix together corn muffin mix, milk, egg, and cream-style corn. Pour into the baking pan.

Once the onions have cooled to room temperature, stir in the sour cream and ½ cup grated cheese. Spread the onion mixture on top of the cornmeal batter. Use the tines of a fork to even it out if necessary. Top the onion mixture with the remaining ½ cup grated cheese. Bake for about 45 minutes, until the top is beginning to brown. Leave out 5 minutes or so before attempting to cut – it is very gooey when hot.

Portuguese Sweet Bread

Nancy's note: This recipe slipped in under the wire as the cookbook was in final editing stages. It is a bread my mother often makes for my kids, and when Tim heard it hadn't been included in this collection, he was appalled. "It's the best bread in the world!" he exclaimed. I said it might seem strange to include just one yeast bread. "The book is supposed to be a collection of our favorites, and this is definitely my favorite," he insisted. So here it is.

Makes 2 spiral loaves

¼ cup warm water
2 packages yeast
1 cup milk
½ cup butter
1 teaspoon salt
4 eggs
¾ cup sugar
6 cups flour
2-3 teaspoons sugar

Pour water into a large bowl and sprinkle yeast over the surface.

In a small saucepan, scald the milk. Add butter and salt, stir to blend, and cool to lukewarm.

In a medium mixing bowl, beat 3 of the eggs with the sugar. Add milk mixture to eggs; then stir this mixture into the yeast/water mixture.

Add 3 cups of the flour. Beat 2 minutes with mixer. Then add about 3 cups more flour, to make a soft, pliable dough. When dough becomes too thick for beater, mix by hand.

Knead on a lightly floured surface until smooth, about 5 minutes. Cover and let rise in a greased bowl for 1 ½-2 hours.

Punch dough down and divide in half. Roll each half into a rope; coil to form a spiral shape; and fit into greased round 9" cake pans. Cover with a dish towel and let rise 1 hour.

Preheat oven to 350°F. Beat remaining egg slightly and brush over loaves. Then sprinkle each one with 1 teaspoon sugar. Bake for 30-40 minutes. Let cool for about 5 minutes; then unmold onto a cookie rack.

Pumpkin Bread

Nancy's note: With so many ingredients now available year-round, there's still something special about recipes you save for certain seasons. This pumpkin bread, from a classic Betty Crocker cookbook, is my family's favorite way to enjoy the flavors associated with autumn baking. My mother remembers using the same recipe when she was a teenager.

Makes 2 large loaves

2/3 cup butter, at room temperature
2 2/3 cups sugar
4 eggs
15-ounce can pumpkin
2/3 cup water
3 1/3 cups flour
2 teaspoons baking soda
1½ teaspoons salt
½ teaspoon baking powder
1 teaspoons ground cinnamon
1 teaspoon ground cloves
2/3 cup chopped walnuts (optional)

Preheat oven to 350°F. Grease two 9 x 5 inch loaf pans.

In a large bowl, cream butter and sugar until fluffy. Stir in eggs, pumpkin and water.

In a medium bowl, mix flour, baking soda, salt, baking powder and spices. Add dry ingredients to pumpkin mixture and mix gently until well-combined.

Pour into greased pans and bake about 1 hour. Let cool 5 minutes; then unmold onto a cookie rack.

Herb Bread

Carolyn's note: I keep on hand in the refrigerator or freezer a supply of herb butter ready to spread between slices of French bread or atop pita or naan. The recipe is approximate and flexible; I never use quite the same ingredients twice. It calls for dried herbs, but if you have fresh ones, so much the better. Use your judgment regarding amount. It always tastes good!

Makes 2-3 long loaves of French bread or the equivalent

1 cup unsalted butter, at room temperature
1 tablespoon finely chopped onion or shallot
½ teaspoon dried tarragon
¼ teaspoon each dried thyme, dried rosemary, and dried sage
2 tablespoons fresh parsley
1 tablespoon grated Parmesan
1 teaspoon Dijon mustard
2-3 French bread loaves or other bread

Preheat oven to 350°F.

Cream butter with all remaining ingredients. Spread on slices of bread.

Lay slices in a single layer on a baking sheet. Bake for about 15 minutes.

To do ahead, butter slices of bread (reshape into a loaf if that's the kind of bread you are using), wrap in foil, and freeze.

Cottage Cheese Pancakes

Nancy's note: These pancakes are moist and rich, with a very different texture from traditional pancakes. My kids (and most of their cousins) like this kind better. More savory than sweet, they are best eaten plain, not with syrup.

Serves 4

1 cup cottage cheese
4 eggs
½ cup flour
¼ cup melted butter or vegetable oil
½ teaspoon salt

Whirl all ingredients in food processor or blender. Prepare a skillet with nonstick spray or melted butter. Fry pancakes until lightly browned, about 3 minutes per side.

Swedish Crêpes

Carolyn's note: My sister Mary Dominick, of Aspen, Colorado, contributed this recipe, which she likes to serve for Sunday breakfast or as light supper with salad.

Serves 4

6 eggs
1 cup flour
2 tablespoons sugar for a sweet filling; 1 tablespoon sugar for a savory filling
1 pinch salt
2 cups milk
2 teaspoons vanilla
Fillings such as yogurt, jam, marmalade, or Nutella for a sweet crêpe; fresh vegetables, ham or bacon, and cheese for a savory crêpe

Preheat oven to 200°F.

In a large mixing bowl, beat eggs. Then add flour, sugar, and salt and mix until no lumps remain. Add milk and vanilla.

Lightly oil a flat skillet or crêpe pan. Pour in about ¼ cup of batter and slide pan around until batter forms a very thin layer. When bubbles form and edges are firm, flip and brown on other side.

Slide crêpe onto plate and keep warm in oven while you finish making remaining crêpes.

Spread each crêpe with the filling of your choice and fold it over. Serve immediately.

SOUPS

Bavarian Cabbage Soup

Carolyn's note: This is one of my favorite winter soups. The seasonings make it interesting but not overly spicy. Additionally, it is lighter than most cabbage soups. Serve it very hot.

Serves 6-8

2 tablespoons extra virgin olive oil
1 medium onion, chopped
1 small cabbage, shredded (about 1 pound)
¼ cup sugar
6 cups consommé or broth (use beef unless you are making a vegetarian
 soup)
1 teaspoon salt
½ teaspoon coarsely ground pepper
½ teaspoon celery seed
1/8 teaspoon dried dill weed
1/8 teaspoon dried rosemary
¼ cup fresh lemon juice
Several shakes Tabasco
4 ounces dried noodles, cooked and drained
1/3 cup sherry

In a large soup pot, heat olive oil. Sauté onion and cabbage over low heat for about 20 minutes. Add sugar, stirring constantly. When cabbage looks glazed, add broth or consommé. Cover and simmer for 30 minutes.

Add salt, pepper, herbs, lemon juice, and Tabasco. Simmer 15 minutes. Stir in noodles and sherry.

Cold Curried Tomato Soup

Carolyn's note: This is one of my favorite summer soups. It takes almost no time to put together.

Serves 6

1 cup plain Greek yogurt
3 cups tomato juice
1 tablespoon extra virgin olive oil
1 tablespoon red wine vinegar
Juice of ½ lemon
1 ½ teaspoons curry powder
3 tablespoons minced onion
¼ teaspoon salt
¼ cup chopped parsley
¼ cup minced chives
¼ teaspoon Tabasco

Blend all ingredients by hand, or mix in a food processor or blender.

Make several hours ahead so that flavors blend.

Serve chilled.

Cold Spinach Soup

Carolyn's note: Cold Spinach Soup is a favorite warm-weather mainstay in our family. The original recipe came from one of my oldest friends, Kari.

Makes about 4 servings

3 cups water
10-ounce package frozen chopped spinach, thawed and drained; or 1
    pound fresh spinach, chopped
1 teaspoon salt
¼ teaspoon black pepper
Juice of 1 fresh lemon
1 teaspoon Worcestershire sauce
1 small onion, minced
1 cup sour cream
1 egg, hardboiled and chopped

Place water, spinach, and salt in a medium saucepan and bring to a boil. Turn off heat. Stir in pepper, lemon juice, and Worcestershire sauce.

Let soup cool to room temperature. Stir in onion, sour cream and egg.

Serve chilled.

Judy's Lentil Soup

Carolyn's note: This soup recipe comes from my cousin Judy Pick Eissner, who can be counted on for cooking that is both flavorful and nutritious.

Serves about 10

1 cup dried lentils
2/3 cup uncooked brown rice
¼ cup vegetable oil
4 cloves garlic, minced
¼ cup soy sauce
4 dried bay leaves
10 cups water
2 large onions, chopped or diced
4 carrots, peeled and diced
2 celery stalks with leaves, diced
28-ounce can diced tomatoes, with liquid
1 cup tomato juice or V-8 juice
2 teaspoons dried basil
1 teaspoon each dried marjoram, thyme, chili powder
1 tablespoon salt
½ teaspoon pepper
1 pound fresh spinach, torn into bite-sized pieces

Put lentils, rice, vegetable oil, garlic, soy sauce, bay leaves, and 6 cups water in a large soup pot. Bring to a boil and simmer for 15 minutes.

Add 4 cups more water along with onions, carrots, celery, tomatoes, tomato juice, basil, marjoram, thyme, chili powder, salt, and pepper.

Cover and simmer for 30 minutes or until vegetables are tender. Stir in spinach leaves. Serve hot.

Oyster Stew

Carolyn's note: Traditionally, I like to serve oyster stew on Christmas Eve, but I usually can't resist making it at other times of year as well.

Serves 4

2 pints fresh oysters in their liquid
¼ cup butter
½ teaspoon salt
½ teaspoon celery salt
1/8 teaspoon pepper
2 cups light cream or half-and-half
1 cup milk
2 tablespoons sherry (optional)
Paprika
Chopped parsley
Oyster crackers

Drain oysters, reserving liquid.

Heat butter in a large skillet. Add oysters; cook about 5 minutes or until edges begin to curl.

Add seasonings, cream, milk, and oyster liquid. Heat over medium heat, just until bubbles form around edge of pan. Do not boil. Add sherry, if using.

Sprinkle with paprika and chopped parsley. Serve with oyster crackers.

Southwestern Pumpkin Soup

Nancy's note: This is another wonderful way to use the savory spices associated with autumn. I make it for nearly every get-together I attend between mid-October and Thanksgiving.

Serves 4-6

3 cups chicken or vegetable broth
1 cup whipping cream
15-ounce can pumpkin
3 tablespoons (packed) dark brown sugar
1 teaspoon ground cumin
½ teaspoon chili powder
½ teaspoon ground coriander
1/8 teaspoon ground nutmeg

Bring broth and whipping cream to boil in heavy medium pot. Whisk in canned pumpkin, brown sugar, cumin, chili powder, coriander and nutmeg.

Reduce heat to medium and simmer until soup thickens slightly and flavors blend, about 15 minutes.

Season to taste with salt and pepper. (Soup is best if prepared several hours and or even a day ahead and left to thicken and mellow.)

Serve hot.

Turkey Chowder

Carolyn's note: Turkey soup can taste like little more than a rehashing of Thanksgiving leftovers. But this soup has enough flavor and texture to seem like a whole new dish – even just a day or two after Thanksgiving. Throw leftover vegetables, stuffing, gravy, and whatever else is around into the pot as well.

Serves 8

4 slices bacon, fried crisp (reserve 2 tablespoons drippings)
1 large onion, sliced
2 large thin-skinned potatoes, peeled and diced
3 cups leftover turkey meat, cut into small pieces
16-ounce can corn, with liquid
16-ounce can stewed tomatoes, with liquid
1 teaspoon salt
¼ teaspoon pepper
4 cups turkey or chicken broth
12-ounce can evaporated milk (regular or skim)
Handful of chopped parsley

Crumble bacon and set aside.

Sauté onion and potatoes in the reserved bacon fat until softened, 10-15 minutes.

Add turkey, corn, tomatoes, salt, pepper, and broth and simmer, covered, for about 20 minutes.

Stir in evaporated milk, crumbled bacon and chopped parsley. Heat thoroughly and serve.

SALADS & SIDE DISHES

Chicken Pasta Caesar Salad

Carolyn's note: This is a flavorful, substantial salad, ideal for a luncheon or a summer dinner. I got this recipe from my friend and former neighbor, Didi.

Serves 4-6

1 pound boneless chicken breasts (or shrimp)
8 ounces dried medium-sized pasta such as penne or rotini, cooked and drained
1 tablespoon extra virgin olive oil
1 head Romaine lettuce
¼ cup light mayonnaise
¼ cup plain yogurt
½ cup Caesar salad dressing, either homemade or a high-quality store-bought brand
½ cup grated Parmesan
1 each large red pepper, yellow pepper, and green pepper, sliced
Salt and pepper

Preheat oven to 375°F. Line a baking pan with foil and spray with nonstick spray.

Layer chicken breasts in pan and brush with some of the Caesar salad dressing. Bake about 15-20 minutes, until cooked throughout. Cool to room temperature; then cut into bite-sized pieces.

Stir together mayonnaise, yogurt, remaining Caesar salad dressing, and Parmesan. In a large salad bowl, toss lettuce, chicken along with its cooking juices, and peppers with mayonnaise mixture. Refrigerate until chilled, about 1 hour.

Just before serving, toss with dressing. Season with salt and pepper to taste.

Cole Slaw

Carolyn's note: Cole slaw is the essence of simple summer flavors. This recipe makes a classic version.

Serves 4-6

¼ cup light mayonnaise
¼ cup sour cream
3 tablespoons cider vinegar
2 teaspoons sugar
1 teaspoon dry mustard
½ teaspoon salt
dash pepper
5 cups shredded cabbage (about 1 pound)

Whisk together all ingredients except cabbage. Once well blended, toss with cabbage.

Crunchy Cole Slaw with Asian Flavors

Nancy's note: I discovered this recipe at a cookout hosted by our former neighbors Cheryl and Craig and was immediately hooked; in fact, I don't remember eating anything else at that cookout! It has the same cruciferous texture as conventional cole slaw but without the heavy mayonnaise flavor. This is another dish for which guests almost always request the recipe.

Serves 8-10

½ cup extra virgin olive oil
2 tablespoons sugar
2 tablespoons unseasoned rice vinegar
2 tablespoons soy sauce
3-ounce package Ramen noodle soup mix
2 tablespoons sesame seeds
½ cup slivered almonds
3 10-ounce bags shredded cole slaw-style cabbage
1 bunch scallions, sliced

Whisk together 6 tablespoons olive oil, sugar, rice vinegar and soy sauce in a small bowl. Set aside.

Lightly chop dried Ramen noodles into small pieces, or break them up by hand. Discard enclosed seasoning packet.

Heat remaining 2 tablespoons olive oil in a medium skillet over medium heat. Cook sesame seeds until just starting to brown; set aside. In the same pan, cook noodles and almonds together until lightly toasted. Set aside to cool.

In a large salad bowl, combine cabbage and scallions; then add noodles, nuts and sesame seeds and lightly toss to combine. Pour dressing over the salad and gently toss again. Serve as soon as possible.

Carolyn's Essential Salad Dressing

Nancy's note: I insisted that my mother write down this recipe, and my children seconded the motion. We all love salad the way she makes it, and none of us can quite replicate it. Using this recipe comes close, though. This is a versatile vinaigrette that works well with any combination of leafy greens and other fresh vegetables.

Makes ¾ cup (easy recipe to increase)

½ cup extra virgin olive oil
¼ cup good quality vinegar, any type
1 teaspoon dry mustard
½ teaspoon salt
1/8 teaspoon pepper
Pinch of sugar
1 clove garlic, minced

Place all ingredients in a jar and shake well. Shake again when ready to use. Store unused dressing in refrigerator.

Aunt Ruth's Broccoli Ring

Nancy's note: When our cousin, Jan Ettlinger Tymorek, of Madison, Wisconsin, heard about our cookbook project, she sent along this family recipe from her grandmother, Ruth Stein Nath, who was my maternal grandfather's elder sister.

Serves 8

2 pounds fresh broccoli
1 clove garlic
2 tablespoons butter
2 tablespoons flour
1 cup heavy cream
4 eggs, separated
salt and pepper

Preheat oven to 350°F. Butter and flour a baking ring or a 2-quart baking dish or soufflé dish.

Place broccoli in a large pot of salted water along with garlic clove. Heat to boiling and cook until tender, about 5 minutes. Discard garlic clove. Drain broccoli and chop coarsely.

In a large mixing bowl, beat egg whites until stiff peaks form.

In a large saucepan, melt butter. Add flour and whisk to combine. Gradually pour in cream. Cook until thickened, about 3 minutes, then whisk in egg yolks and broccoli. Set aside to cool. When room temperature, fold in stiffly beaten egg whites and season with salt and pepper.

Pour into baking ring. Place ring in pan of hot water and bake for 30 minutes.

Serve with Quick Hollandaise Sauce (recipe on p. 99).

Tabbouleh

Nancy's note: When I was a sophomore in high school visiting a friend one summer day, my friend's mother made tabbouleh from a mix. I suppose my perspective was a bit distorted; I couldn't believe anyone would bother to use a mix rather than just make it from scratch. I went home and made a batch of tabbouleh to bring over to my friend's family, hoping to enlighten them. I can't imagine being so forward now, but I'm glad I know how to make tabbouleh.

Serves 6

1 cup bulgur
2 cups water
½ cup chopped parsley
½ cup chopped red onion
1/3 cup freshly squeezed lemon juice
1/3 cup extra virgin olive oil
2 cloves garlic, minced
2 medium tomatoes, diced
½ cup diced green pepper
¼ cup pignolia nuts
½ cup frozen peas, thawed
2 tablespoons chopped fresh mint
2 teaspoons grated lemon zest
1 teaspoon salt
½ teaspoon cayenne pepper

Put bulgur in a medium mixing bowl and cover with water. Soak at least one hour. Drain, and press out extra water with the back of a large spoon.

Toss bulgur with all remaining ingredients. Chill several hours or overnight.

Tuna and Bulgur Salad

Nancy's note: This salad tastes particularly good in the summer, made with fresh mint and ripe tomatoes. The addition of tuna, providing protein, makes it well-balanced enough to serve as an entrée for a lunch or light supper.

Serves 6

1 cup bulgur
2 cups water
4 celery stalks, diced
6 scallions, sliced
¾ cup fresh parsley, chopped
¾ cup fresh mint, chopped
¼ cup cured black olives (such as Kalamata), pitted and chopped
1 cup cherry tomatoes or grape tomatoes, halved
2 cans tuna, drained and flaked with a fork
1/3 cup lemon juice
1/3 cup extra virgin olive oil
1 clove garlic, minced
Salt and pepper to taste

Put bulgur in a medium mixing bowl and cover with water. Soak at least one hour. Drain, and press out extra water with the back of a large spoon.

Toss bulgur with all remaining ingredients. Chill several hours or overnight.

Danish Cucumbers

Carolyn's note: This is definitely the "go-to" vegetable for our whole family. Almost any entrée goes well with Danish cucumbers.

Serves 6

3 large cucumbers, peeled and thinly sliced
2 teaspoons salt
3 tablespoons extra virgin olive oil
2 tablespoons rice vinegar
2 tablespoons water
1-2 tablespoons fresh chopped dill or ½ teaspoon dried dill
2 teaspoons sugar

Place cucumber slices in a colander and toss with salt. Set aside to drain about 20 minutes.

In a small mixing bowl or glass measuring cup, whisk together olive oil, vinegar, water, dill, and sugar. Toss with cucumber slices. Set aside to marinate for at least 2 hours and up to 6 hours if possible.

Roasted Winter Squash

Nancy's note: Winter squash is one cooked vegetable my kids have always been happy to eat. Dressed up with olive oil, garlic, and Parmesan in this preparation, it's hardly even recognizable as the nutritious, vitamin-packed vegetable it really is.

Serves 6

2 pounds winter squash (butternut or acorn), peeled and cut into
    medium-sized cubes
2/3 cup flour
1 teaspoon salt
¼ teaspoon pepper
1/3 cup grated Parmesan
2 cloves garlic, cut into slivers
1/3 cup extra virgin olive oil

Preheat oven to 425°F.

In a one-gallon plastic bag, combine flour, salt, and pepper. Add squash pieces to the bag and shake to dredge, until each piece of squash is coated in flour.

Put squash cubes in a single layer in a well-greased 9" x 13" baking pan.

Sprinkle with grated Parmesan and slivered garlic. Drizzle with the olive oil.

Bake for 45 minutes.

Roasted Cauliflower

Carolyn's note: Even with all our modern conveniences and technology, New England winters are long, cold, and dark. Roasting vegetables adds warmth and flavor to a drab winter evening.

Serves 4-6

1 large head of cauliflower, separated into bite-sized florets
3 tablespoons extra virgin olive oil
¼ teaspoon salt
Freshly ground pepper to taste
3 tablespoons balsamic vinegar
½ cup finely shredded Parmesan

Preheat oven to 450°F. Line a large rimmed baking sheet with foil.

Toss cauliflower, olive oil, salt, and pepper in a large bowl. Spread in a single layer on the baking sheet.

Bake until cauliflower starts to soften and brown on the bottom, 15 to 20 minutes.

In a large bowl, toss the cauliflower with vinegar and sprinkle with cheese. Return it to the baking sheet and roast in the oven until the cheese is melted and any moisture has evaporated, 5 to 10 minutes more. This is equally delicious served hot or at room temperature.

Italian Roasted Vegetables

Nancy's note: This is such a simple concept, and yet it's another one for which guests always ask for the recipe. It goes well as a side dish for any kind of meat or fish, and is also popular at a dinner potluck. The ingredients are flexible; use whatever vegetables you have on hand.

Serves about 6

2 large bell peppers, any color, cut into strips
2 medium onions, cut into rings
2 medium to large tomatoes, cut into wedges
½ pound mushrooms, sliced
½ cup black olives, halved
½ cup dry breadcrumbs or Panko
½ teaspoon salt
¼ teaspoon black pepper
½ teaspoon dried basil (or 1 tablespoon fresh, chopped)
½ teaspoon dried oregano (or 1 tablespoon fresh, chopped)
½ cup extra virgin olive oil
3 tablespoons red wine vinegar
1 clove garlic, minced
½ teaspoon salt

Preheat oven to 350°F.

In a 9" x 13" baking pan sprayed with nonstick spray, arrange vegetables in a single or slightly overlapping layer.

In a small mixing bowl, mix breadcrumbs, salt, pepper, and herbs; sprinkle over vegetables. In a small mixing bowl or glass measuring cup, whisk together olive oil, red wine vinegar, garlic, and salt; then drizzle over vegetables and crumbs.

Bake for about 35 minutes. Serve hot or at room temperature.

Oven-Baked Rice

Carolyn's note: Rice cookers are a very popular kitchen item these days, but you can also make rice in the oven. Unlike a stovetop method, this recipe requires no attention at all to the rice once you've mixed the ingredients, so you can let it bake while you prepare other parts of the meal.

Serves 6

1 ½ cups uncooked white rice
3 cups water
1 teaspoon salt
3 tablespoons butter

Preheat oven to 350°F.

Combine ingredients in a 2-quart casserole with a cover.

Bake, covered, for 50-60 minutes, until liquid is absorbed, stirring once or twice.

Before serving, fluff up rice with a fork.

Orange Rice

Carolyn's note: Orange rice is tangy and savory; it goes well with fish or chicken.

Serves 6-8

1 ½ cups uncooked white rice
2/3 cup diced celery
3 tablespoons butter
2 tablespoons grated orange rind
½ cup dried apricots, diced
¾ cup orange juice
2 cups water
1 teaspoon soy sauce
1 teaspoon celery seed
1 ½ teaspoon salt

Preheat oven to 350°F.

Gently toss together all ingredients in a large mixing bowl. When well combined, pour into a large greased casserole with a tight-fitting cover.

Bake, covered, 1 hour.

Fried Rice

Carolyn's note: This is a basic fried rice recipe. Add whatever vegetables you have on hand to the onions, peas and carrots.

Serves about 6

2 tablespoons sesame oil
1 tablespoon vegetable oil
1 small onion, minced
½ cup frozen peas, thawed
½ cup diced carrots
1 clove garlic, minced
2 eggs, lightly beaten
2-3 cups <u>cooked</u> rice (brown or white)
3 tablespoons soy sauce
1 teaspoon oyster sauce
1 teaspoon sriracha or another hot sauce
1 scallion, sliced

Heat oils together in a wok, Peking pan or skillet. Stir-fry onion, peas, carrots, and garlic until slightly softened, about 5 minutes.

Push vegetables to one side of the pan. Pour in eggs. Cook until set; then lightly scramble. Mix in vegetables.

In a small mixing bowl, combine soy sauce, oyster sauce, and sriracha. Toss with vegetables.

Stir in cooked rice and heat thoroughly. Top with sliced scallion.

Dried Cherry Pilaf

Carolyn's note: This pilaf goes especially well with duck or goose.

Serves 6-8

½ cup dried cherries
½ cup dry red wine
2 tablespoons extra virgin olive oil
1 small onion, chopped
1½ cups combination of uncooked wild rice and uncooked long grain rice
2 cups chicken broth
1 cup water
1 teaspoon salt
1 teaspoon dried rosemary (or 2 teaspoons fresh rosemary)
3 scallions, sliced
¼ cup pecans, chopped and toasted

Mix cherries with wine in a microwaveable bowl or glass measuring cup; microwave for about 2 minutes. Set aside.

In a large skillet, sauté onion in olive oil. Add rice; stir for about 5 minutes. Add cherries with liquid to rice.

Add broth, water and seasonings to skillet. Simmer over medium-low heat until liquid is absorbed. (Alternatively, transfer mixture to a casserole; bake at 350°F for about 45 minutes or until liquid has been absorbed.) Fluff with fork. Stir in scallions and pecans.

Didi's Potatoes

Nancy's note: This approach to preparing potatoes comes from our former next door neighbor, Didi. It is a very good dish to bring to a potluck – it travels well, it can be served hot or room temperature, and nearly everyone likes it.

Serves 4-6 (Easy to double or triple)

6 large red or yellow thin-skinned potatoes, cut into quarters
½ cup extra-virgin olive oil
2 tablespoons rice wine vinegar
2 tablespoons fresh lemon juice
2 cloves garlic, minced
1 teaspoon Dijon mustard
1 tablespoon chopped fresh herbs such as tarragon, oregano, or rosemary, or a combination
¾ cup grated Parmesan

Preheat oven to 350°F. Spray a 9" x 13" baking dish with nonstick spray.

Whisk together oil, vinegar, garlic, mustard, herbs, and ½ cup Parmesan.

Put the quartered potatoes in a large mixing bowl and pour in dressing. Stir to coat all sides of potatoes. Pour potatoes in a single layer into baking dish. Sprinkle with remaining ¼ cup grated Parmesan.

Bake for about an hour, until tender and starting to brown (longer is fine too). Serve hot or at room temperature.

Potato Pancakes

Nancy's note: From a nutritional standpoint, it's hard to justify eating potato pancakes. But it's also tough to give them up forever! So we wait until December and draw upon our Jewish ancestry to claim we need potato pancakes, or latkes, to help us celebrate the Hanukah season. Once a year doesn't seem like such a bad thing.

Serves 4

2 large potatoes, peeled
1 egg, lightly beaten
1 tablespoon flour
½ teaspoon salt
1/8 teaspoon pepper
1 pinch ground nutmeg
About ¼ cup vegetable oil for frying

Grate potatoes with a hand grater or the grating blade of a food processor. Place in a colander, weigh down with a plate, and set aside to drain for about 30 minutes.

In a large bowl, toss potatoes with egg, flour, salt, pepper, and nutmeg.

Heat oil in heavy skillet. Drop batter by large spoonfuls into the skillet; flatten gently with spatula.

Fry about 3 minutes on each side or until golden brown.

Drain well on paper towels. Serve with sour cream or applesauce, or both!

Yorkshire Pudding

Carolyn's note: Yorkshire Pudding, very much like a popover, is an old-fashioned British recipe that is traditionally served with roast beef. I think the most authentic recipes use beef fat, but I substitute butter. Generous amounts of pepper and nutmeg create a savory flavor.

Serves 8

1½ cups flour
1 teaspoon salt
1 teaspoon pepper
1 teaspoon ground nutmeg
4 eggs, beaten
1½ cups milk
½ cup butter

Mix flour, salt, pepper, and nutmeg in a medium mixing bowl. In a saucepan, heat milk until little bubbles form around edges of pan.

With an electric mixer, beat eggs into dry ingredients one by one; then add hot milk in small increments, stirring after each addition, until it is all well combined.

Cover bowl with a dish towel and chill batter for about 2 hours.

Preheat oven to 450°F. While the oven is heating, put butter in a 9" x 13" baking dish and put the dish in the oven to let the butter melt. When the oven has finished preheating, take the batter out of the refrigerator; beat it again, and then pour it over the melted butter in the baking dish. Bake 15 minutes; then reduce heat to 300°F without opening oven door and bake 15 minutes longer. Serve hot.

BEEF, LAMB, PORK, POULTRY & SEAFOOD

Cider Pot Roast

Carolyn's note: Most often, I think of preparing a braised dish like this in the late fall or winter. It's good any time of year. Cider gives it a special New England flair. Carrots and onions may be added to the dish during the last hour of simmering.

Serves about 8

3-4 pounds chuck roast of beef
1½ cups cider
1 tablespoon brown sugar
2 teaspoons kosher salt
¼ teaspoon ground cinnamon
¼ teaspoon ground ginger
2 whole cloves
6 tablespoons flour
¼ cup vegetable oil
2 tablespoons water

Place beef in a large bowl. In a small mixing bowl, mix cider, sugar, salt and spices. Pour over beef and refrigerate for at least 24 hours and up to two days. Turn beef occasionally.

Remove meat from marinade. Sprinkle it all over with about 4 tablespoons flour. Heat oil in a Dutch oven or large soup pot with a cover. Brown beef on all sides in hot oil. Turn heat to low; add marinade to pot, cover and simmer for 3 hours.

Remove roast to large casserole or serving piece. Slice.

On stove, dissolve remaining 2 tablespoons flour in water. Stir into marinade. Cook and stir for about 5 minutes to thicken the gravy.

Pour some of the gravy onto meat and serve the remainder from a gravy boat.

Mill Iron Farm Hamburgers

Carolyn's note: Much as we all like to test out interesting new dishes, we also like basic preparations, especially when it comes to showcasing the flavor of our homegrown Mill Iron Farm organic beef. I do the mixing and seasoning, and Dick does the grilling. This is our favorite way to prepare hamburgers.

Makes 4-6 burgers, depending on size

1 slice sandwich bread
¼ cup milk
1 pound lean ground beef
1 egg
1 teaspoon salt
¼ teaspoon pepper
1 teaspoon Worcestershire
¼ cup catsup

In a medium bowl, pour milk over bread. Let soak for a few minutes.

Add remaining ingredients. Mix it as gently as you can with your hands. The less you handle the mixture, the lighter and more tender it will taste. Shape into 4-6 patties.

Heat and oil your grill or a skillet. Cook the patties about 4 minutes per side.

Greek-Style Lamb Burgers

Carolyn's note: Mill Iron Farm is known for its organic beef, but some years we've raised a sheep or two as well, which has given us the chance to experiment with lamb or mutton recipes. Here's one of my favorites.

Makes about 6 burgers, depending on size

1½ pounds ground lamb or mutton
1 small onion or 2 shallots, finely chopped
2 cloves garlic, minced
3 tablespoons chopped fresh mint or 2 teaspoons dried mint
1 teaspoon dried oregano
1 teaspoon salt
½ teaspoon black pepper

With hands, mix all ingredients together until well combined. Form into 6 patties about ½ -inch thick.

Heat and oil your grill or a skillet. Cook the patties about 4 minutes per side. Serve on grilled pita bread rounds.

Good garnishes for lamb burgers include lettuce, thinly sliced red onion, Feta, and tzatziki.

Pineapple Barbecue Pulled Pork Sandwiches

Nancy's note: Both of my sisters are terrific cooks. My older sister Lauren tends to choose more complicated methods; my younger sister Sarah favors straightforward recipes that almost anyone can follow. I like to eat what Lauren makes, but I like to receive recipes from Sarah. She sent me this one because we both like using our crock pots.

6-8 servings

1 (2-3 pound) boneless pork shoulder
¼ cup brown sugar
1 teaspoon chili powder
1 teaspoon paprika
1 teaspoon salt
¼ teaspoon black pepper
2 cloves garlic, minced
½ cup pineapple juice
1 cup barbecue sauce, plus more for serving
6-8 hamburger buns

Place pork shoulder in a lightly greased crock pot.

In a small bowl, combine brown sugar, chili powder, paprika, salt, and pepper. Sprinkle over the pork.

In another small bowl, stir together the minced garlic, pineapple juice and barbecue sauce. Pour over the pork.

Cook on low for 6-8 hours, or until the meat shreds easily with a fork.

Shred the pork and serve on hamburger buns. Top with additional barbecue sauce, if desired.

Baked Apricot Chicken

Nancy's note: I made up this recipe to serve to guests on a gluten-free diet. Risotto is good as a side dish.

Serves 6-8

½ cup apricot jam
3 tablespoons lemon juice
2 tablespoons tamari
2 cloves minced garlic
2 tablespoons Dijon mustard
1 tablespoon extra virgin olive oil
4-6 large boneless chicken breasts, halved

In a small mixing bowl, whisk together jam, lemon juice, tamari, garlic, mustard, and olive oil. Place chicken breasts in a single layer in a baking dish and pour the marinade over. Chill, marinating, for 2-24 hours, turning chicken pieces and basting with sauce occasionally.

Preheat oven to 350°F. Bake about 20 minutes.

Chicken Casserole

Nancy's note: This is a great way to use up cooked chicken (or turkey). It has an uncomplicated taste that appeals to all kinds of eaters. All amounts are approximate; just use what you have.

Serves 4-6

2 cups cooked, diced chicken
1 cup diced celery
½ cup diced red or yellow pepper
½ cup slivered almonds, toasted
¼ cup sliced black olives
2 tablespoons minced onion or shallots
¾ cup light mayonnaise
1 teaspoon Italian seasoning
1 teaspoon Worcestershire sauce
Juice of 1 lemon
½ teaspoon salt
¼ teaspoon pepper
1/3 cup dried breadcrumbs or Panko
1/3 cup grated Parmesan

Preheat oven to 350°F.

Mix all ingredients except breadcrumbs and Parmesan together and place in a greased 9" x 13" baking dish. Mix breadcrumbs and Parmesan and sprinkle over the casserole.

Bake about 25 minutes.

Slow-Roasted Garlic and Lemon Chicken

Carolyn's note: There are myriad ways to prepare baked chicken. When I tasted this dish, I decided that I had found the perfect recipe. Lemons and garlic are two of my favorite ingredients; I use them in so many of the dishes that I prepare.

Serves 4–6

1 chicken (3½ to 4 pounds), cut into about 10 pieces
1 head garlic, separated into unpeeled cloves
2 unwaxed lemons, cut into chunky eighths
2 tablespoons fresh thyme or 1 teaspoon dried
3 tablespoons extra virgin olive oil
¾ cup white wine
Salt and pepper to taste

Preheat oven to 300°F.

Put the chicken pieces into a roasting pan and add the garlic cloves, lemon chunks, and thyme. Add the oil and mix everything with your hands; then spread the mixture out, making sure all the chicken pieces are skin-side up.

Sprinkle the white wine, salt, and freshly ground pepper over the chicken; then cover tightly with foil and put in the oven to cook for 2 hours.

Remove the foil from the roasting pan, and turn up the oven to 400°F. Cook the uncovered chicken for another 35–45 minutes, by which time the skin on the meat will have turned golden brown and the lemons will have begun to scorch and caramelize at the edges.

Serve hot, warm, or cold. I like it best served warm.

Chicken Stir-Fry

Carolyn's note: This is a Szechuan-style dish but isn't nearly as spicy as many traditional Szechuan recipes. Meat or tofu could be substituted for chicken. Stir-fries are a good way to use up various vegetables that have collected in your garden or refrigerator.

Serves 4-5

1 pound boneless chicken, cut into strips or cubes
6-8 cups assorted fresh vegetables such as peppers, carrots, celery, mushrooms, and scallions, cut into bite-sized or smaller pieces

Marinade
1 tablespoon cornstarch
1 tablespoon sherry
1 tablespoon soy sauce
2 cloves garlic, minced
2 teaspoons minced fresh ginger

Sauce
½ cup chicken or vegetable broth
2 teaspoons cornstarch
¼-½ teaspoon crushed red pepper flakes
1 teaspoon sesame oil
2 tablespoons soy sauce
2 tablespoons hoisin sauce (optional)
3 tablespoons wine vinegar
1 tablespoon sugar
3 tablespoons vegetable oil
½ cup peanuts or cashews

In a small bowl, mix marinade ingredients. Marinate chicken pieces in a 1-gallon plastic bag or baking dish, refrigerated, for 30-60 minutes.

In a medium bowl or glass measuring cup, stir together sauce ingredients.

Heat 2 tablespoons oil in a wok or large skillet over medium heat.

Stir-fry chicken pieces until they turn white and can easily be cut, about 3 minutes. Remove chicken and put aside.

If wok is dry, add another tablespoon of oil to the pan and heat. Stir-fry vegetables until tender-crisp, about 4-5 minutes.

Return chicken to wok. Add sauce mixture and stir until the mixture is hot and the sauce has thickened.

Sprinkle nuts on top.

Serve with rice.

Pat's Turkey Loaf

Carolyn's note: My sister Pat Spitzmiller, who lives in Dillon, Colorado, sent me this recipe. Serve it with a salad for a relatively low-fat and very satisfying dinner.

Serves 4

1 pound ground turkey
1 cup herbed stuffing mix
1 egg, slightly beaten
½ cup chopped onion
1 tablespoon horseradish
½ teaspoon dry mustard
¼ cup milk
1/3 cup light mayonnaise
½ cup dried cranberries

Preheat oven to 375°F. Spray a 9" x 5" loaf pan with nonstick spray.

Mix all ingredients together and press into loaf pan. Bake about 1¼ hours.

Pour off grease and let stand a few minutes before serving.

Baked Fish with Mustard Sauce

Carolyn's note: When we are vacationing in Maine, we buy fish from a local harborside fish market just hours after it has been caught. Fish as fresh as that calls for the simplest kind of preparation, so I often turn to this recipe.

Serves 6

2 pounds fresh fish fillets
½ cup light mayonnaise
¼ cup Dijon mustard
1 small onion, finely diced
1 tablespoon soy sauce
½ cup dry breadcrumbs or Panko

Preheat oven to 425°F. Spray a 9" x 13" baking pan with nonstick spray.

In a medium mixing bowl, combine mayonnaise, mustard, onion, and soy sauce.

Place fish pieces in single layer in baking pan. Spread sauce evenly over the fish.

Sprinkle top with breadcrumbs. Bake about 20 minutes or until fish flakes easily. (Amount of time depends on thickness of fish.)

Serve with lemon wedges.

Mediterranean Fish Stew

Carolyn's note: This favorite recipe is a basic fish stew. Any kind of white fish can be used. Of course, shellfish can be added, too. Serve over white or brown rice.

Serves 4

3 tablespoons extra virgin olive oil
1 large onion, chopped
2 cloves garlic, minced
½ cup chopped celery
½ cup diced green pepper
½ pound mushrooms, sliced
2 1-pound cans diced tomatoes with their juice (or 2 pounds fresh tomatoes if in season)
½ cup white wine
8-ounce bottle clam juice
½ cup minced parsley
Salt and pepper to taste
1 pound fresh fish or shelled, deveined shrimp or a combination

In a large soup pot, heat olive oil. Sauté onion, garlic, celery, green pepper, and mushrooms over medium heat until soft, about 6-8 minutes.

Add tomatoes with their juice, white wine, and clam juice. Simmer for about 30 minutes. Add parsley.

Add fish and continue simmering at medium heat about 10 more minutes or until fish flakes. If using shrimp, add it in the last 5 minutes of simmering.

Shrimp and Scallop Posole

Carolyn's note: Posole is a traditional Mexican dish that has been adopted and adapted all over the world. Traditionally it uses meat (generally pork) rather than seafood. I like this variation.

Serves 4

2 tablespoons extra virgin olive oil
1 cup chopped onion
3 cloves garlic, chopped fine
3 8-ounce bottles clam juice
½ cup white wine
1 can (about 15 ounces) white hominy, drained and rinsed
1 cup mild tomatillo salsa (or any green salsa)
Grated peel and juice from 1 lime
1 teaspoon dried oregano
1 teaspoon ground cumin
3 tablespoons diced sundried tomatoes
1 pound uncooked shrimp, peeled and deveined
1 pound sea scallops, halved horizontally
¼ cup chopped parsley

In a large soup pot or Dutch oven, sauté onion and garlic until tender, about 5 minutes. Add clam juice, wine, hominy, salsa, lime juice, oregano, cumin, and sundried tomatoes. Simmer 20 minutes.

Add seafood and parsley. Cook about 5 minutes, until shrimp and scallops are opaque.

Season with salt and pepper to taste.

> **Garnishes that go well with posole:**
>
> Lime wedges
> Sliced radishes
> Diced red peppers
> Minced scallions or onions
> Chopped cilantro
> Baked tortilla strips

Crab Cakes

Carolyn's note: The trick with crab cakes is to use the bare minimum of seasonings and binding ingredients in order to let the flavor of the crabmeat shine through. I think this is just the right balance of crabmeat and other flavors.

Serves 6

1 pound fresh crabmeat
1 egg, beaten
¼ cup light mayonnaise
¼ cup minced onion
½ cup buttery cracker crumbs (such as Ritz)
1 teaspoon grated lemon
½ teaspoon Worcestershire
½ teaspoon dry mustard
¼ teaspoon salt
¼ teaspoon cayenne pepper
2 tablespoons butter
2 tablespoons extra virgin olive oil
6 lemon wedges

Gently mix all ingredients except butter, olive oil and lemon wedges. Drain off any liquid, and form into about six patties the size of small hamburgers.

Refrigerate on a baking sheet to firm up, about 30-60 minutes.

In a large skillet, heat oil and butter together. When melted, sauté crab cakes about 2-3 minutes per side. Serve immediately, topped with lemon wedges.

VEGETARIAN ENTREES

Almost Lasagna

Nancy's note: This is a variation on lasagna, using the same principle but with a different taste. Many years ago, when our neighbors, Rob and Cindy, came home from the hospital with their new baby, Emily, I brought this dish over and was flattered when they asked for the recipe. Eighteen years later, I happened to run into Cindy the day before Emily was leaving for her first year at college. Cindy told me that she was making Emily's favorite dish for that night's farewell dinner – "almost lasagna"!

Serves 8

1 pound rotini, ziti or other medium-sized dried pasta, cooked and drained
2 cups tomato sauce, homemade or store-bought
8 ounces cream cheese, at room temperature
8 ounces sour cream
1 teaspoon salt
¼ teaspoon ground pepper
1 teaspoon dried oregano
2 cups shredded Monterey Jack
½ cup shredded Parmesan

Preheat oven to 350°F. Spray a 9" x 13" baking dish with nonstick spray.

In a large mixing bowl, blend together cream cheese, sour cream, salt, pepper, oregano, Parmesan, and 1 cup Monterey Jack.

Toss pasta with cream cheese mixture until well coated. Spread into baking dish. Spread tomato sauce over the pasta, then top with remaining 1 cup Monterey Jack.

Bake for 30 minutes. Turn on the broiler for the last 5 minutes to brown the top.

Creamy and Savory Mac & Cheese

Nancy's note: Many macaroni and cheese recipes are too bland for most adult palates, but this version is richly textured with interesting flavors, based on whatever kind of cheese you have on hand. Moreover, it's a great way to use up those random scraps and shards of cheese that tend to accumulate in the refrigerator.

Serves 8

16 ounces rotini, ziti or other medium-sized dried pasta, cooked and drained
¼ cup butter
¼ cup flour
½ teaspoon salt
¼ teaspoon black pepper
1/8 teaspoon cayenne pepper
1/8 teaspoon ground nutmeg
2¾ cup milk
1 pound assorted cheeses, grated – I like to use about 4 ounces each of Cheddar, Monterey Jack, Parmesan and Mozzarella, but you can use bits of whatever kind you have on hand
½ cup dried breadcrumbs or panko

Preheat oven to 350°F. Spray a 9" x 13" baking dish with nonstick spray.

In a large saucepan, melt the butter over medium heat. Keeping the heat on, whisk in the flour, stirring constantly for about 2 minutes until it is well blended into the butter. Mix in spices.

Heat the milk to a simmer. Add it to the butter and flour mixture in a slow steady stream, whisking continuously. Heat the mixture, stirring frequently, until it thickens slightly, about 3 minutes. Add cheese and stir over low heat until cheese is all melted.

Place pasta in a large bowl. Pour cheese sauce over it and mix gently until all the pasta is well coated. Pour the pasta into the baking dish. Sprinkle breadcrumbs or panko over the top.

Bake about 30 minutes, until heated throughout. Serve immediately.

Pasta with Cherry Tomatoes and Arugula

Nancy's note: After buying organic homegrown garlic from our neighbors at the Farmers Market, I made up this recipe to show off its pungent flavor. The slight crunch of the garlic and almonds contrasts beautifully with the silky arugula and cherry tomatoes.

Serves 4

12 ounces rotini, penne or other medium-sized dried pasta, cooked and drained (save about ¼ cup cooking water as you drain it)
¼ cup extra virgin olive oil
4-6 cloves garlic, thinly sliced
¼ cup sliced blanched almonds
1 pint cherry tomatoes
10 ounces fresh arugula
¼ cup Kalamata olives, pitted
Ground black pepper to taste

Heat olive oil in large skillet. Sauté garlic and almonds together over medium heat until both are just starting to brown.

Turn heat to medium-low and add cherry tomatoes to the same pan. Heat, stirring occasionally, until tomatoes start to split, about 6-8 minutes. As tomatoes split, mash them gently with the back of a fork or mixing spoon.

Once all the tomatoes have split and been lightly mashed, stir in olives, arugula, and reserved pasta water. Heat about 5 more minutes, until arugula is thoroughly wilted.

Season with ground pepper and serve over hot pasta, or simply add the cooked pasta to the skillet, turn off heat, and toss gently before serving.

Skillet Gnocchi with Tomatoes, White Beans and Greens

Nancy's note: Since most of us try for lighter cuisine these days, I feel compelled to justify the heartiness of this dish. When I share this recipe, I usually say something like "It's perfect after a day of skiing, snowshoeing, or working outside in the cold." What I mean by that is that it's definitely substantial fare. Until I tried this recipe, I had never heard of this technique of preparing gnocchi by sautéing rather than boiling it, but strangely enough, it works!

Serves 6

2 tablespoons extra virgin olive oil
16-ounce package dried gnocchi (<u>not</u> the fresh refrigerated kind)
4 cloves garlic, minced
½ cup water
10 ounces frozen spinach, kale or Swiss chard, thawed and well-drained
15-ounce can diced tomatoes, drained
15-ounce can white beans, drained
¼ teaspoon ground black pepper
½ cup shredded mozzarella
¼ cup finely shredded Parmesan

Heat 1 tablespoon oil in a large skillet over medium heat. Add gnocchi and cook, stirring often, without letting it stick to the pan, until gnocchi plumps up and starts to brown. This takes about 8-10 minutes. Transfer to a bowl.

Add the remaining tablespoon of oil to the pan and sauté the minced garlic about 3 minutes. Stir in the water and the spinach, kale, or chard and cook, stirring, until combined. Add tomatoes, beans, and pepper and bring to a simmer. Then add the gnocchi and sprinkle in the cheese. Heat until the cheese is melted and the sauce is bubbling. Serve immediately.

Pad Thai

Nancy's note: I've liked Pad Thai ever since I first tasted Thai food in college. Although I don't know how authentic this preparation is, my whole family enjoys it, and it adds variety to our weeknight menus. If you don't want a vegetarian version, add some cooked chicken or shrimp.

Serves 6-8

8 ounces dried wide rice noodles
3 cloves garlic, minced
¼ cup fish sauce
3 tablespoons brown sugar
1 ½ tablespoons ketchup
3 tablespoons rice vinegar
½ cup water
4 ounces button mushrooms, whole
4 ounces fresh green beans or peapods
8 ounces broccoli florets
¼ cup vegetable oil
2 eggs, lightly beaten
4 ounces bean sprouts
¼ cup peanuts

Heat a kettle of water to boiling. Place rice noodles in a large bowl and pour boiling water over. Set aside for 20-30 minutes to soften.

In a medium mixing bowl or large glass measuring cup, whisk together garlic, fish sauce, brown sugar, ketchup, rice vinegar, and water.

In a steamer or large pot, steam the mushrooms, green beans or peapods, and broccoli florets for about 3 minutes.

Heat 2 tablespoons vegetable oil in a wok or Peking pan. Break eggs into the hot oil and let them start to set; then scramble them. Once the eggs are cooked, add the steamed vegetables and toss together. Then add bean sprouts and peanuts.

Drain the rice noodles and add those to the wok. Pour sauce over the noodles and vegetables, toss to combine, and heat thoroughly at low heat.

Corn, Veggie, and Grain Casserole

Nancy's note: This is another substantial vegetarian casserole, full of tasty vegetables, grains and nuts.

Serves 6

1 ½ cups corn kernels, fresh or frozen
½ cup pine nuts, toasted
2 ½ cups <u>cooked</u> short-grain brown rice
14-ounce can artichoke hearts, drained
4-ounce can chopped jalapeños, drained
3 cloves garlic, chopped
10 ounces frozen broccoli, thawed and drained
1 teaspoon ground cumin
1 teaspoon kosher salt
¼ teaspoon ground black pepper
2 tablespoons extra virgin olive oil
8 ounces grated Cheddar

Preheat oven to 375°F.

Line a rimmed baking sheet with foil, spray with nonstick spray, and spread corn kernels in a thin layer. Roast in the oven for about 20-30 minutes, checking often to be sure they don't burn. Stir once in a while since the ones at the edges cook fastest. When some are starting to brown and others are still yellow, take them out.

Place corn in a large mixing bowl. Toss in all other ingredients. Mix gently to combine. Spread into a 9" x 13" baking dish sprayed with nonstick spray. Turn oven down to 350°F and bake about 45 minutes, uncovered. Serve hot.

Vegetable Risotto

Nancy's note: This is more of a ratio than a recipe – the proportions of Arborio rice and broth work well, and then you can add whatever vegetables you like. The way I've written it here reflects my favorite additions and flavors.

Serves 4 as an entree or 6 as a side dish

5 tablespoons extra virgin olive oil
2 tablespoons chopped onion
3 cloves garlic, minced
1 large red, yellow, or orange pepper, diced
1 medium or large zucchini or summer squash, diced
4 cups vegetable broth
¼ cup pine nuts, lightly toasted
2 tablespoons white wine
1 cup uncooked Arborio rice
½ cup grated Parmesan

Heat 2 tablespoons olive oil in a large risotto pan or a skillet with high sides over medium heat. Sauté onion until soft, about 5-6 minutes. Add chopped garlic and cook another 2 minutes. Scrape into a small bowl and set aside.

Heat another tablespoon of olive oil in the same pan and sauté peppers and zucchini or squash until slightly softened, about 5 minutes. Set aside with onions and garlic.

In a medium saucepan, bring the vegetable broth to a simmer and keep it simmering. Heat remaining 2 tablespoons olive oil at medium heat in the same large pan you've been sautéing the vegetables. Pour in Arborio rice and white wine and stir well to combine.

Once wine is absorbed, add 1 cup broth. Keeping the pan over medium heat, stir frequently until broth is absorbed. Then add remaining broth ½ cup at a time, stirring well and allowing each new addition to be fully absorbed before adding the next one. In all, it will take about 25 minutes to use all the broth.

When all the broth has been absorbed, turn heat to low. Add vegetables, pine nuts and parmesan. Stir well and serve immediately.

Spinach Enchiladas

Nancy's note: This has been my son Tim's favorite dinner for as long as I can remember. When he was in first grade, he had an assignment that involved making a chart of all his favorites in various categories: favorite book, animal, vacation spot, ice cream flavor, etc. For "favorite food," he carefully wrote, "Spinish Incholatas." I don't think his teacher knew what he meant, but I did!

Serves 4-6

8 ounces cream cheese, at room temperature
10-ounce package frozen chopped spinach, thawed and drained
1 cup grated Monterey Jack
½ cup crumbled Feta or Queso Fresco
1 packet taco seasoning mix
6 soft flour tortillas
10-ounce can enchilada sauce
1 cup sour cream

Preheat oven to 375°F. Spray a 9" x 13" baking dish with nonstick spray

Beat cream cheese in electric mixer until fluffy. Add spinach, cheeses, and taco seasoning. Mix at medium speed until well combined.

Spread out the flour tortillas one at a time and spread with spinach mixture; then roll up and place in pan. Pour enchilada sauce over the top.

Cover pan with foil and bake for about 30 minutes; then uncover and bake for another 5 minutes.

Serve with sour cream on the side.

Vegetarian Mexican Tortilla Casserole

Nancy's note: This is hearty fare for vegetarians who like Tex-Mex flavors.

Serves 6

1 cup corn kernels, fresh or frozen
¼ cup vegetable oil
1 dozen soft corn tortillas
¼ cup finely chopped onion
3 cloves garlic, minced
15-ounce can diced tomatoes, drained
10-ounce package frozen spinach, thawed and drained
15-ounce can black beans, drained
1 teaspoon ground cumin
1 teaspoon chili powder
1 teaspoon kosher salt
1 small can chopped jalapenos (optional)
½ cup light cream or half-and-half
½ cup crumbled Feta or Queso Fresco
½ cup grated Monterey Jack

Preheat oven to 375°F. Line a rimmed baking pan with foil, spray the foil with nonstick spray, and spread the corn kernels over it in a thin layer. Roast in the oven for about 20-30 minutes, checking often to be sure they don't burn. Stir once in a while since the ones at the edges cook fastest. When some are starting to brown and others are still yellow, take them out.

Heat the vegetable oil in a very large skillet or a large soup pot. Tear the corn tortillas into about 6-8 pieces each and sauté them in the oil until they are crisp. This takes about 10 minutes. As soon as each piece is crisp, remove from the pan, lay it on a plate covered with a paper towel to drain off the oil and then set aside in a bowl.

Once you're done cooking the tortillas, use the same pan to sauté the onion and garlic until soft but not yet brown, about 5 minutes. (There should still be enough oil to prevent the onions from sticking, but if not, add a couple tablespoons more.) Then add the canned tomatoes, spinach, black beans, and roasted corn kernels and heat to a simmer.

Add cumin, chili powder, salt, cream, chopped jalapenos and cheese. Heat and stir until the cheeses are melted and the whole mixture is hot but not boiling.

Stir in tortilla pieces and serve immediately.

Spanakopita (Greek Spinach and Cheese Pie)

Nancy's note: This is a vegetarian entrée that nearly everyone savors, and it works equally well at brunch, lunch, or dinner. Working with phyllo dough is somewhat time-consuming and messy, but the results are delicious and impressive. If you want to save time and don't care about maintaining the recipe's ethnic authenticity, use puff pastry in place of phyllo dough: put one layer on the bottom and one on the top, and skip the brushing with melted butter.

Serves 8

½ pound phyllo dough, at room temperature
1 medium onion, diced
1 cup butter, melted
3 10-ounce packages frozen spinach, thawed and well-drained
3 eggs, beaten
1 cup ricotta
8 ounces crumbled Feta
1 teaspoon dried dill or 2 tablespoons fresh dill
1 teaspoon salt
1/8 teaspoon pepper
Juice of ½ lemon

Preheat oven to 450°F.

In a large skillet, sauté onion in ¼ cup melted butter until soft. Turn off heat. Add spinach to skillet.

In a medium mixing bowl, combine eggs, ricotta, feta, dill, salt, pepper, and lemon juice. Stir this mixture into the spinach.

Brush a 9" x 13" baking dish lightly with melted butter. Unroll phyllo dough and place one sheet in casserole. Brush it lightly with butter. Repeat this step seven more times. Pat spinach mixture evenly over phyllo layers. Then layer eight more phyllo layers on top of the spinach, brushing each layer lightly with butter.

Trim the uneven edges of phyllo dough and cut the pie into 12 squares. Then bake it for 10 minutes. Reduce heat to 350°F and bake another 45 minutes. Let sit about 10 minutes before serving.

Pissaladière (French Pizza)

Carolyn's note: This is our very loose interpretation of the dish from the south of France known as pissaladière. A savory treat for a brunch or light supper, it is easy to make and looks enticing, with its bright colors.

Serves 6-8, depending on how large the slices are cut

1 sheet frozen puff pastry, thawed
2 tablespoons Dijon mustard
½ cup grated Parmesan
1 onion, thinly sliced
2 large tomatoes, thinly sliced and drained
Zucchini, summer squash, peppers, mushrooms, or other fresh vegetables
2 teaspoons dried oregano (or 2 tablespoons fresh)
½ cup shredded Mozzarella

Preheat oven to 425°F. Line a rimmed baking sheet with parchment paper.

Roll the puff pastry into an approximately 12" x 16" rectangle. Slide it onto the parchment paper. Pinch the edges into a rim. Prick the pastry at 1-inch intervals with a fork. Bake for 10 minutes.

Spread pastry with mustard. Sprinkle with Parmesan, then arrange vegetables over the pastry. Sprinkle oregano over the top, then top with Mozzarella.

Bake about 25 minutes more. Serve hot or warm.

Thai Red Lentil Stew

Nancy's note: I don't know how authentic the "Thai" claim is, but the unusual flavors in this delicious vegetarian stew make it taste not quite like anything else I make. I like to prepare a batch on the weekend and pack it for brown-bag lunches all week. Like most soups and stews, the flavors seem to improve the longer it sits.

Serves 6-8

2 tablespoons extra virgin olive oil
1 large yellow onion, diced
1 red bell pepper, seeded and diced
3 cloves garlic, minced
2 tablespoons chili powder
1 large sweet potato, diced
1 cup dried red lentils
1 teaspoon salt
4 cups vegetable broth
½ cup dried barley
15-ounce can kidney beans, drained
2 tablespoons Thai red curry paste
15-ounce can lowfat coconut milk
28-ounce can diced tomatoes, drained
¼ cup fresh cilantro, plus extra for garnish (optional)

In a large soup pot, sauté onions and pepper in oil over medium heat until partially softened, about 5 minutes. Add garlic and sauté a minute more.

Add chili powder, sweet potato pieces, lentils, salt, vegetable broth and barley. Cover and bring to a boil. Let boil for 15 to 20 minutes, stirring occasionally to prevent burning.

When lentils are cooked and sweet potatoes are tender, add the remaining ingredients and heat through. If possible, let sit for an hour or more before serving.

West African Vegetable Stew

Nancy's note: Once again, I feel compelled to add the disclaimer that I can't vouch for the ethnic authenticity of this dish, but I do love the flavors and textures of the vegetables, sweet potato, chick peas and peanut butter combined.

Serves 8-10

2 tablespoons extra virgin olive oil
1 medium onion, chopped
1 large sweet potato, diced
2 cloves garlic, minced
1 medium zucchini, diced
2 carrots, peeled and diced
¾ teaspoon dried thyme
¼ teaspoon ground cumin
6 cups vegetable broth
¾ cup uncooked white rice
15-ounce can diced tomatoes, undrained
2 16-ounce cans chick peas, drained
1/3 cup peanut butter, chunky or smooth
Salt and pepper to taste

Heat olive oil in a large soup pot or Dutch oven. Add onion, sweet potato, garlic, zucchini, and carrots and sauté until slightly softened, about ten minutes. Stir in thyme and cumin.

Add vegetable broth and rice. Cover pot and simmer about 15 minutes. Add tomatoes and chick peas. Heat to boiling. Add peanut butter. Stir until peanut butter is dissolved. Turn off heat and leave soup to cool to room temperature.

Take out about 2 cups of the soup and place in blender or food processor. Blend until smooth; then stir back into soup pot. Season with salt and pepper to taste. If possible, let soup sit for a couple of hours or more before serving so flavors may blend.

SAUCES & MARINADES

Three Easy Marinades

Carolyn's note: We like to grill all year round, and because we raise our own cattle, we have access to what we consider the world's most delicious beef. In the summer, we use our outdoor firepit; in the cooler months we use the indoor fireplace in our kitchen. Here are three of my favorite marinades for making good beef taste even better. All of these versions work best if the meat is left to marinate in them for several hours.

Each recipe makes enough for 2-3 pounds of meat

Steak Marinade I

1/3 cup vegetable oil
¼ cup soy sauce
3 tablespoons honey
2 tablespoons red wine vinegar
1 scallion, sliced
1 clove garlic, minced
1 ½ teaspoons ground ginger

Put all ingredients in a jar; shake well.

Steak Marinade II
(even easier)

½ cup orange marmalade or apricot jam
¼ cup soy sauce
¼ cup lemon juice

Stir ingredients together.

Steak Marinade III

½ cup soy sauce
1/3 cup sherry
1/3 cup brown sugar
¼ cup vinegar
2 tablespoons vegetable oil
1 clove garlic, minced
½ teaspoon ground ginger

Put ingredients in a jar and shake.

Jocie's Mustard

Carolyn's note: Especially now with fewer people willing to indulge in cookies and candy over the holidays, lower-fat edible gifts like this are particularly appreciated. This homemade condiment can be used on ham or turkey sandwiches, with pretzels, or as a dip for fresh vegetables, to name just a few possibilities.

Makes about 1 ½ cups. Pack in small jars; a little goes a long way.

¾ cup packed light brown sugar
4-ounce tin Coleman's mustard powder
1 cup good quality apple cider vinegar
¼ cup honey
3 large eggs, beaten

Whisk brown sugar and mustard powder in a metal mixing bowl to combine. Add vinegar and honey; whisk well. Strain through a fine mesh sieve into a large metal bowl. Add eggs and whisk until blended.

Set bowl with mustard mixture over a large saucepan of gently simmering water. Be sure bottom of bowl is not touching water. Cook, whisking and scraping bottom of bowl frequently, until mustard is thick and a thermometer registers 160°F, about 5 minutes.

Divide among jars. Cover and chill. Mustard can be kept refrigerated for up to 2 months.

Fresh Mint Sauce

Carolyn's note: This sauce goes especially well with lamb. Mint is an easy (almost too easy!) herb to grow during summer months.

Makes a little over 2 cups

1 cup water
1 cup cider vinegar
2 cups sugar
¼ teaspoon salt
1 cup firmly packed fresh mint leaves
Few drops green food coloring (optional)

In a medium saucepan, mix water, vinegar, sugar, and salt. Bring to a boil, stirring constantly. Boil hard for three minutes.

Add mint leaves. Remove from heat. Let cool to room temperature.

Let the mixture stand at room temperature overnight. Then remove the mint leaves and place them in a sieve over the liquid. Gently pound the mint leaves with a heavy spoon to "bruise" the leaves and release the flavor. Discard mint leaves.

Add a few drops of food coloring if you want a characteristic mint-green hue; omit this step if you don't mind a slightly cloudy sauce. Refrigerate. Sauce will keep for several months.

It is easy to increase the amount of sauce.

Quick Hollandaise Sauce

Carolyn's note: This sauce is especially good with steamed asparagus or artichokes. Although it isn't a classic Hollandaise, it makes an easy substitute.

Makes 1/3 cup or about 4 servings

¼ cup light mayonnaise
1 tablespoon fresh lemon juice
2 tablespoons butter
1 egg yolk
1 dash salt
1 dash cayenne pepper

In top of a double boiler over low heat, combine mayonnaise and lemon juice. Blend well. Let cook 3 minutes, or until warm throughout.

Add butter and egg yolk. Stir constantly over low heat until mixture thickens. Add salt and cayenne pepper. Remove from heat.

COOKIES & CANDY

Chocolate Crackles

Carolyn's note: I often freeze the balls of dough before baking. They are ready to pop into the oven at a moment's notice.

Makes about 3 dozen cookies

½ cup butter, at room temperature
2 cups sugar
4 ounces unsweetened chocolate, melted
4 eggs
2 teaspoons vanilla
2 cups flour
2 teaspoons baking powder
½ teaspoon salt
1 cup confectioner's sugar

In a large mixing bowl, cream butter and sugar together. Add melted chocolate, eggs, and vanilla.

In a medium mixing bowl, combine flour, baking powder, and salt. Stir into chocolate mixture. Chill dough at least 2 hours.

Preheat oven to 350°F. Line a cookie sheet with parchment paper.

Roll dough into 1-inch balls and then roll each ball in confectioner's sugar. Bake on cookie sheet 12 minutes, or until edges are firm and center is still soft. (If you choose to freeze the balls of dough, add a few minutes to the baking time.) Cool for about 5 minutes, then remove to a cookie rack.

Eddie Elephant Cookies

Nancy's note: This is a soft chocolate cookie studded with chocolate chips. When my father was a child, he had a favorite picture book in which Eddie the Elephant packed up chocolate cookies for an excursion through the jungle. I'm not sure how he determined these were these exact cookies, but that's why we call them "Eddie Elephant Cookies."

Makes about 3 dozen cookies

½ cup butter, at room temperature
1 cup sugar
1 egg
1 ¾ cups flour
½ teaspoon salt
½ teaspoon baking soda
½ cup unsweetened cocoa
¾ cup buttermilk (or mix 1 tablespoon white or cider vinegar into
    ¾ cup milk)
1 cup chocolate chips

Preheat oven to 400°F. Line a cookie sheet with parchment paper.

In a large mixing bowl, cream together butter and sugar. Blend in egg.

In a medium mixing bowl, combine flour, salt, baking soda, and cocoa. Add dry ingredients to butter mixture. When well combined, mix in buttermilk and chocolate chips.

Drop by rounded teaspoons onto cookie sheet. Bake for about 8 minutes, until edges are firm. Cool for about 5 minutes, then remove to a cookie rack.

Ginger Molasses Cookies

Carolyn's note: This is an old-fashioned cookie with a sweet, spicy flavor and a chewy texture.

Makes about 3 ½ dozen cookies

1 ½ cups flour
2 teaspoons baking soda
½ cup oatmeal
1 teaspoon ground cinnamon
1 teaspoon ground ginger
¼ teaspoon ground cloves
½ teaspoon salt
¾ cup butter, melted
1 ½ cups sugar, plus some for rolling
¼ cup molasses
1 egg

In a medium mixing bowl, combine flour, baking soda, oatmeal, spices, and salt.

In a large mixing bowl, mix melted butter with sugar, molasses, and egg. Add dry ingredients and mix until well-combined.

Chill dough for at least two hours.

Preheat oven to 350°F. Line a baking sheet with parchment paper.

Shape dough into 1" balls and roll in remaining sugar. Place on cookie sheet, well-spaced (cookies will spread as they bake). Bake for 10 minutes. Cool for about 5 minutes, then remove to a cookie rack.

Oatmeal Chocolate Chip Cookies

Nancy's note: I've often remarked that writing and baking cookies are my only two skills, so if I ever give up journalism, I guess I'll have to become a pastry chef. This is the recipe I turn to most often: these cookies are foolproof and popular with everyone. Because it has no eggs, the dough can be consumed unbaked without worry – which can be an advantage or a disadvantage, depending on your perspective.

Makes about 3 dozen cookies

1 cup butter, at room temperature
1 cup brown sugar
1 cup flour
1 teaspoon baking soda
½ teaspoon salt
1 teaspoon vanilla
2 cups raw oatmeal (old-fashioned or quick)
1 cup chocolate chips

Preheat oven to 350°F. Line a cookie sheet with parchment paper.

Cream together butter and brown sugar. In a small mixing bowl, combine flour, baking soda and salt. Add dry ingredients to butter mixture.

Then add vanilla, oatmeal and chocolate chips and mix thoroughly.

Drop by teaspoonfuls onto cookie sheet and bake for 10 minutes. Cool for about 5 minutes, then remove to a cookie rack.

Peanut Butter Chocolate Chip Cookies

Nancy's note: I'm a fool for traditions, no matter how mundane. And somehow the tradition evolved that when the kids have "snow days," I always make peanut butter chocolate chip cookies. (However, if you ask Tim, he will say the tradition is for me to make bacon on snow days. Somehow I think the cookies are actually the healthier option.)

Makes about 3 dozen cookies

½ cup butter, at room temperature
½ cup peanut butter (smooth or chunky, but use a supermarket brand,
    not natural or fresh-ground)
½ cup white sugar
½ cup brown sugar
1 egg
1¼ cups flour
¾ teaspoon baking soda
½ teaspoon baking powder
¼ teaspoon salt
1 cup chocolate chips (I like milk chocolate chips for this recipe)

Preheat oven to 375°F. Line a cookie sheet with parchment paper.

In a large mixing bowl, cream together butter, peanut butter, and sugars. When well blended, add egg.

In a small mixing bowl, combine flour, baking soda, baking powder, and salt. Stir dry ingredients into butter mixture. Add chocolate chips.

Drop by teaspoonfuls onto cookie sheet. Bake 10 to 12 minutes, until edges are firm. Cool for about 5 minutes, then remove to a cookie rack.

Reverse Chocolate Chip Cookies

Nancy's note: At some point this recipe appeared on the Nestlé white chocolate chips package, though I haven't seen it there in a while. Every year for our school fundraising auction, I offer a "cookies-of-the-month" item. Each month, the winning bidder receive two dozen cookies – their choice of what kind. The last family to win this asked for these cookies the first month – and then requested them again every month thereafter. I kept urging them to try something new, but they weren't budging!

Makes about 3½ dozen cookies

1 cup butter, at room temperature
¾ cup white sugar
2/3 cup brown sugar
2¼ cups flour
1 teaspoon baking soda
½ teaspoon salt
2/3 cup unsweetened cocoa
2 eggs
1 cup white chocolate chips

Preheat oven to 350°F. Line a cookie sheet with parchment paper.

In a large mixing bowl, cream together butter and both sugars. In a medium mixing bowl, combine flour, baking soda, salt, and cocoa. Mix dry ingredients into butter mixture; then add eggs and combine well. Mix in white chocolate chips.

Drop dough by teaspoonfuls onto cookie sheet and bake 8 minutes. The cookies may look or feel slightly underbaked when you take them out, but that's fine. Leave them on the cookie sheet about 3 minutes to set, then move onto a cookie rack to cool.

Holly Cookies

Nancy's note: Whatever the opposite of gourmet is would describe these cookies. Marshmallows, food coloring....honestly, we're a little embarrassed. And yet, resembling dark green wreaths with little red berries, they add such a striking effect to a holiday cookie assortment, plus they taste delicious! We think of them as a guilty pleasure and realize it's good that Christmas comes around only once a year.

Makes about 2½-3 dozen

½ cup butter
10-ounce package marshmallows
1 teaspoon vanilla
5 cups cornflakes
Several drops green food coloring

Line a cookie sheet with waxed paper and spray with nonstick spray.

Melt butter and marshmallows together. Add the vanilla and cornflakes. By drops, add enough food coloring to turn the mixture green.

Drop by medium-sized spoonfuls onto cookie sheet. Press a couple of cinnamon dots into each one to look like holly berries. Cool at room temperature, then refrigerate until ready to serve.

Meringue Cookies

Nancy's note: Meringues are a light and crunchy novelty. For Easter, we use a couple of drops of food coloring to tint them in pastel shades.

Makes about 3 dozen cookies

3 egg whites, at room temperature
15 tablespoons sugar (one cup minus one tablespoon)
1 teaspoon vanilla
½ cup mini chocolate chips (optional)

Preheat oven to 350°F. Line a cookie sheet with parchment paper.

Using an electric mixer, beat egg whites until foamy. Gradually add sugar, beating until mixture forms very stiff peaks. Add vanilla and chocolate chips, if using.

Drop by large spoonfuls onto cookie sheet. Put cookies into preheated oven and immediately turn off heat. Leave meringues in oven without opening the door for at least eight hours (overnight is preferable).

Three Kinds of Candy for the Holidays

Nancy's note: Rather than baking cookies at Christmastime, I like to give homemade candy as gifts. It's easy to package in a decorative tin or box and keeps well. Here are three of my favorite candy recipes. Although candy-making can be complicated, these three recipes are easy and almost foolproof.

I. Peanut Brittle (or other nut brittle)

Makes 1¼ pounds

1½ cups peanuts or other nuts
1 cup sugar
½ cup corn syrup
Pinch of salt
1 tablespoon butter
1 teaspoon vanilla
1 teaspoon baking soda

Line a baking sheet with parchment paper or well-greased aluminum foil.

Stir together nuts, sugar, corn syrup and salt in a medium glass bowl or other heavy microwaveable bowl. Microwave at full power 6 minutes.

Quickly stir in butter and vanilla. (Be very careful working with this mixture, as it is extremely hot and sticky.)

Microwave 2 minutes more. Stir in baking soda.

Pour onto baking sheet. Set aside to cool for about 30 minutes. Break into pieces.

II. Peanut Butter Chocolate Candies

Makes about 3 dozen

1½ cups graham cracker crumbs
1 cup confectioner's sugar
½ cup butter, at room temperature
½ cup peanut butter (smooth or chunky)
6 ounces chocolate chips
1 tablespoon butter

Mix together graham cracker crumbs, confectioner's sugar, butter, and peanut butter. Shape into balls about the size of walnuts. Place in a single layer on a cookie sheet spread with waxed paper and refrigerate for an hour or more.

Make glaze by melting chocolate chips and butter together over very low heat, stirring constantly. Then dip one side of each peanut butter ball into glaze. Place back on cookie sheet and refrigerate until glaze has hardened. Freeze until ready to serve.

III.   Toffee

Makes about 1 pound

1 cup butter
1 cup sugar
3 tablespoons water
1 cup chocolate chips

Line a cookie sheet with parchment paper.

In a medium saucepan over medium heat, heat butter, sugar and water. As butter melts, stir constantly until mixture comes to a low boil.

Continue stirring over heat until mixture turns a streaky caramel color (this takes about 15 minutes). Then quickly pour over the pan lined with parchment paper.

Spread mixture fairly thin but without any tears or holes. Let sit five minutes.

Pour chocolate chips over the top. Give the chocolate chips a couple of minutes to melt; then spread evenly over the top with a knife or frosting spatula.

Set aside to cool completely; then break into chunks. Store in the refrigerator or freezer.

Truffles

Nancy's note: ...And one more candy recipe: my favorite. Although these simple chocolates may technically have little in common with the truffles sold at upscale candy shops, they are remarkably popular as holiday gifts or on a dessert table or cookie platter. The recipe comes from the Beany Malone Cookbook, a favorite of ours for the past forty years.

Makes about 4 dozen

1 cup butter
12 ounces chocolate chips
2 cups confectioner's sugar
2 teaspoons vanilla
1 cup unsweetened cocoa

In a medium saucepan over low heat, melt butter and chocolate chips together.

Remove from heat. Sift in confectioner's sugar. Add vanilla and ½ cup cocoa. Stir together until smooth. Set aside to cool until firm enough to form into balls, about 1 hour.

Roll into small balls and then roll each ball in remaining cocoa.

Refrigerate or freeze until ready to use.

Poppycock

Carolyn's note: Many people are familiar with packaged caramel corn, but the taste and texture are much fresher when you make it yourself. A bag or tin of this treat makes an excellent holiday gift.

Makes 3 quarts

12 cups popped popcorn (start with ½ cup unpopped corn)
1 cup mixed nuts, any type (almonds, pecans, peanuts)
¾ cup butter
1 ½ cups brown sugar
1/3 cup light corn syrup
½ teaspoon salt
½ teaspoon baking soda
1 teaspoon vanilla extract

Preheat oven to 250°F. Grease a large rimmed baking sheet.

Combine popcorn and nuts in a large bowl.

Melt butter in a large saucepan over medium heat. Stir in brown sugar, corn syrup and salt. Bring to a boil, stirring constantly. Then allow to boil for 5 minutes without stirring. Remove from heat; stir in baking soda and vanilla.

Pour syrup over ingredients in bowl and stir until the popcorn is well-coated. Spread out on baking sheet.

Bake for 1 hour, stirring every 20 minutes. Let cool to room temperature; then store in airtight container.

DESSERTS

Apple Cake

Carolyn's note: With no need for peeling apples or creaming butter, this cake is quick and easy to make. You can even chop the apple pieces in a food processor (quarter them first, and pulse). It's perfect for a dessert, afternoon tea or with morning coffee.

Makes 9 servings

2 cups diced or chopped apple pieces (no need to peel)
1 cup sugar
1½ cups flour
1 teaspoon baking soda
½ teaspoon salt
½ teaspoon ground cinnamon
1 egg
½ cup vegetable oil
1 teaspoon vanilla
½ cup chopped walnuts or pecans

Topping (optional)
½ cup sugar
3 tablespoons flour
¼ teaspoon ground cinnamon
Pinch of salt
2 tablespoons butter, melted

Preheat oven to 350°F. Grease an 8" or 9" baking pan.

In a medium mixing bowl, stir sugar into apples and let set for 10 minutes. In another medium mixing bowl, combine flour, baking soda, salt, and cinnamon. Stir into apple mixture. Then add oil, egg, vanilla, and nuts. Combine well and pour into baking pan.

In a small bowl, combine all ingredients for topping and sprinkle over batter. Bake 40-45 minutes. Cool about 10 minutes in pan before serving.

Apple Crisp

Nancy's note: Kids love to go apple-picking in the fall. My problem with it is that an hour of fun in the orchards yields about ten times as many apples as anyone will actually eat. So from Columbus Day to Thanksgiving, we make many apple crisps.

8 servings

4 cups sliced apples (peeled or unpeeled), or substitute ½ cup fresh
   cranberries for ½ cup of the apples
1 cup flour
1 cup sugar
1 teaspoon baking powder
1 teaspoon ground cinnamon
½ teaspoon salt
½ teaspoon ground nutmeg
1 egg, slightly beaten
½ cup butter, melted

Preheat oven to 375°F. Place sliced apples into a greased 8" baking dish.

In a small bowl, combine dry ingredients. Then mix in egg with a fork or pastry blender until mixture forms coarse irregular crumbs. Sprinkle crumb mixture over apples.

Drizzle melted butter over the top. Bake for 45 minutes.

Aunt Doris's Blueberry Cake

Carolyn's note: Doris Roberts, Dick's aunt, made this cake the first time we had it. It has become a family favorite. We have made it with apples, pears, plums, raspberries, and blackberries.

Makes about 8 servings

Cake
½ cup butter, at room temperature
1 cup sugar
2 eggs
1 teaspoon vanilla
1 cup flour
1 teaspoon baking powder
¼ teaspoon salt
1 pint blueberries

Topping
1 tablespoon sugar
1 teaspoon ground cinnamon

Preheat oven to 350°F. Grease a 9" pie plate or springform pan.

In a large mixing bowl, cream butter and sugar together. Add eggs and vanilla. Mix well.

In a small bowl, combine flour, baking powder, and salt stir into batter. Spread into pie plate or springform pan. Top with fruit.

For topping, mix sugar and cinnamon together and sprinkle over batter.

Bake for 50 minutes. Cool 15 minutes in pan before unmolding

Chocolate Zucchini Cake

Nancy's note: This chocolate zucchini cake is a fun way to use extra summer produce, though I always feel obligated to explain to the uninitiated why it is full of bright green shards. My sister Lauren claims the recipe works just as well with beets (in which case you have purple shards to explain).

Makes about 12 servings

2½ cups flour
¼ cup unsweetened cocoa
1 teaspoon baking powder
1 teaspoon baking soda
½ teaspoon salt
1 cup brown sugar
½ cup white sugar
½ cup vegetable oil
½ cup buttermilk
3 eggs
1 teaspoon vanilla
1 pound grated uncooked zucchini or grated cooked beets
1 cup chocolate chips

Preheat oven to 350°F. Grease a Bundt pan or 9" x 13" baking pan.

In a large mixing bowl, combine flour, cocoa, baking powder, baking soda, and salt. In a separate large mixing bowl, combine sugars and oil; then mix in buttermilk, eggs, and vanilla.

Add half the flour mixture and stir well to combine. Then add the zucchini or beets. Add the other half of the flour mixture and the chocolate chips. Pour the batter into the prepared pan. Bake 45-50 minutes. Cool 15 minutes in pan before unmolding.

Fudge Almond Torte

Carolyn's note: This recipe has been dubbed "Dick's Birthday Cake" in our family. It is his favorite dessert, and I make it at various times throughout the year – but most definitely for his birthday.

Serves 8

Cake

2 tablespoons strong brewed coffee
4 ounces chocolate chips or other good-quality semi-sweet chocolate, chopped
3 eggs, separated, at room temperature
½ cup butter, at room temperature
¾ cup sugar
2 ounces (¼ cup) crumbled almond paste
½ cup flour

Chocolate Glaze

4 ounces chocolate chips or other good-quality semi-sweet chocolate, chopped
1 tablespoon butter
2 tablespoons slivered almonds, toasted (optional)

Preheat oven to 350°F. Grease a round 8" or 9" cake pan.

In a double boiler or a metal bowl set over a pan of simmering water, melt chocolate. Stir in coffee.

In a large mixing bowl, beat egg whites until soft peaks form.

In another bowl, beat butter and sugar until creamy. Mix in almond paste and egg yolks, one by one.

Gently fold chocolate mixture and then flour into butter mixture.

Fold in beaten egg whites, about one-third at a time.

Spread batter into pan; bake for 30 minutes. Let sit for 5 minutes; then unmold onto a cookie rack.

To make glaze, combine chocolate and butter in a double-boiler or small metal bowl set over simmering water and stir until melted. Cool slightly and spread over cake.

Garnish with slivered almonds.

Chocolate Mousse Pie

Nancy's note: This appealing and very easy dessert is a crowd-pleaser. When Tim was in middle school, word slipped out that it was one of his specialties. A friend made a bet with him about some trivial matter: if Tim won, he'd get five dollars; if the friend won, Tim would make him a chocolate mousse pie. The friend won the bet, and that evening promptly at 7 p.m., the boy's father drove him over to our house to collect.

Serves 8-10

Graham Cracker Crust
1 ¼ cups graham cracker crumbs
¼ cup sugar
5 tablespoons butter, melted

Chocolate Mousse
12 ounces chocolate chips or other good-quality semi-sweet or dark
    chocolate, chopped
3 cups whipping cream
Pinch salt
1 teaspoon vanilla
¼ cup sugar

To make crust, combine melted butter, sugar, and crumbs. Press into a 10" or 12" springform pan which has been greased or lined with waxed paper or parchment paper (it's fine to use waxed paper since you won't be putting it in the oven). Put in the freezer for at least 15 minutes to firm up.

To make mousse, place chocolate in a food processor along with salt and vanilla.

Process the chocolate mixture briefly. In a small saucepan, heat 1 cup of the whipping cream to very hot but not boiling. Pour it into the food processor as the processor is running. Continue processing until mixture is well blended. Set aside to cool for about 10 minutes.

In a large mixing bowl, whip remaining 2 cups cream with sugar until stiff peaks form. Fold the chocolate mixture into the whipped cream until all is well combined. Spread mousse over graham cracker crust and refrigerate for an hour or more before serving.

To serve, open the springform sides and then slide the crust onto a plate or other serving dish.

Chocolate Pistachio Marble Cake

Carolyn's note: With its mixes and chocolate syrup, this is the kind of non-gourmet recipe that never would have shown up in my earlier cookbooks. But again, it's a family favorite, so it gets to appear in this one. It was introduced to us by my sister-in-law, Sandra. The flavors of vanilla, pistachio, and chocolate are delicious, and the cake is so moist it doesn't need any frosting, though if you wanted one, I would recommend the chocolate glaze from the Fudge Almond Torte recipe (page 120).

Serves 10-12

1 package yellow cake mix (if possible, find one that does *not* say
    "pudding in the mix")
1 package instant pistachio pudding mix
3 eggs
1 cup water
1/3 cup vegetable oil
½ cup Hershey's chocolate syrup

Preheat oven to 350°F. Grease a Bundt pan, a 9" x 13" baking pan, or two 9" cake pans.

In a large mixing bowl, mix together cake mix, pudding mix, eggs, water, and oil. Pour two-thirds of batter into prepared pan.

Add chocolate syrup to remaining batter and mix well. Swirl chocolate batter over pistachio batter. (No need to mix in; it will marble in as it bakes.)

Bake about 45-50 minutes. Leave in pan about 15 minutes to cool before unmolding.

Chocolate Bread Pudding

Nancy's note: Several years ago, my mother and I collaborated to prepare a meal for a multi-generational family that was gathering for a memorial service. We thought the whole meal looked enticing, but every time we've run in to anyone from this family since then, they remind us specifically of how much they enjoyed this dessert

Serves 8

4 cups white bread, slightly stale if possible, cubed or torn into small
   pieces
3 cups half-and-half
½ cup sugar
1/8 teaspoon salt
10 ounces chocolate chips or other good-quality semi-sweet or dark
   chocolate, chopped
6 large eggs
1 teaspoon vanilla

Grease a 2 ½ - to 3-quart soufflé dish. Place bread pieces in dish. In a medium saucepan, heat half-and-half, sugar, and salt over medium heat, stirring, until sugar is dissolved and mixture is hot but not boiling. Remove from heat and add chocolate, then let stand two minutes. Whisk until smooth. Lightly beat eggs together in a large bowl and slowly add chocolate mixture, whisking until combined. Stir in vanilla. Pour mixture over bread and let soak at room temperature, pressing bread down occasionally, 1 hour.

Preheat oven to 325°F. Fill a 9" x 13" baking dish or other large dish that your soufflé dish will fit into with about 1 inch water. Place the soufflé dish into the water bath and put into the oven. Bake until edge is set but center still trembles slightly, about 1-1 ¼ hours. Set aside to cool at least 20 minutes before serving – pudding will continue to set as it cools. Serve warm. You might wish to top servings with vanilla ice cream or whipped cream.

Cocoa Angel Pie

Carolyn's note: Way back in the 1970s, I supplied a quaint country store in the nearby town of Lincoln, Massachusetts, with a small number of prepared dishes. This was one of my most popular offerings. The filling is similar to a light chocolate mousse, but the crust is an unusual and surprisingly tasty meringue mixture.

Serves 6

Crust
1 cup sugar
1 teaspoon baking powder
3 egg whites
23 Ritz crackers, crushed
½ cup pecans, chopped
1 teaspoon vanilla

Filling
1 cup heavy cream
2 tablespoons unsweetened cocoa
3 tablespoons sugar

Preheat oven to 350°F. Grease or spray a 9-inch pie plate.

In a small mixing bowl, combine sugar and baking powder. With electric mixer, beat egg whites until stiff, gradually add the sugar mixture. Fold in crushed crackers, nuts and vanilla. Spoon into pie plate. Bake for 25 minutes. Set aside to cool.

Whip heavy cream, adding cocoa and sugar slowly as you beat, until soft peaks form. Spread over cooled crust. Refrigerate for at least an hour before serving.

Garnish with grated chocolate and whipped cream, if desired.

Eggnog Cheesecake

Nancy's note: This is another seasonal recipe – I dream of it eleven months of the year and then finally make it for as many events and parties as I can once December rolls around!

Serves 8-10

Crust
5 tablespoons butter, melted
1 ¼ cups graham cracker crumbs
¼ cup sugar

Filling
3 8-ounce packages cream cheese, at room temperature
1 cup sugar
3 tablespoons flour
¾ cup eggnog
2 eggs
2 tablespoons rum (optional)
1 pinch ground nutmeg

Make crust by combining butter, graham cracker crumbs, and sugar. Press into an 8" or 9" springform pan which has been greased or lined with parchment paper. Freeze for at least 15 minutes to firm up.

Preheat oven to 425°F. In a food processor or blender, combine cream cheese, sugar, flour and eggnog; process until smooth. Blend in eggs, rum (if using) and nutmeg. Pour mixture into crust. Bake for 10 minutes. Reduce heat to 250°F and bake for 45 minutes more, or until center of cake is barely firm to the touch. Let cake cool completely before removing the springform rim (chilling it overnight is best).

Mud Pie Cake

Nancy's note: In a way, mud pie cake was the original inspiration for this cookbook. Throughout her teen years and well into her twenties, my sister Lauren had frequent opportunities to do homestay programs in Europe. It became a family joke that no sooner did she land in a European family's house – and kitchen – than she was calling home for the recipe for mud pie cake. It's the kind of family recipe we all pass back and forth over and over again (and really, Lauren should have just sewn it into a pocket in her suitcase). Mud pie cake is a dark chocolate cake so moist it doesn't need frosting – just a dusting of powdered sugar or nothing at all. (Moreover, if you want to make a cake-loving vegan happy, this is the cake to make!)

Serves 8-10

1½ cups flour
3 tablespoons unsweetened cocoa
1 teaspoon baking soda
1 cup sugar
½ teaspoon salt
5 tablespoons vegetable oil
1 tablespoon cider vinegar
1 teaspoon vanilla
1 cup cold water

Preheat oven to 350°F. Grease an 8" or 9" round or square baking pan.

In a medium or large mixing bowl, combine dry ingredients. Then stir in the liquid ingredients one at a time, mixing well after each addition.

Pour the batter into the prepared pan. Bake for 30 minutes.

Cool for 15 minutes and then unmold.

Nantucket Cranberry Pie

Carolyn's note: Sylvia Goodwin, Dick's cousin who lives in Marblehead, shared this favorite recipe. She wrote that every autumn, her family asks her to make this pie (which is more like a cake).

Serves 8

2 cups fresh (or frozen) cranberries
½ cup walnuts or pecans, coarsely chopped
1½ cups sugar
¾ cup butter or margarine, at room temperature
2 eggs, slightly beaten
1 teaspoon almond extract
1 cup flour
¼ teaspoon salt

Preheat oven to 325°F. Spray a 10" pie plate with nonstick spray.

Put cranberries into pie plate. Sprinkle nuts and then ½ cup sugar over the cranberries.

In a medium mixing bowl, beat together butter and remaining 1 cup sugar. Add eggs and almond extract. Mix until well blended. Stir in flour and salt.

Spread batter over cranberries. Bake for 60 minutes.

Serve warm as is, or top with ice cream or whipped cream.

Pots de Crème

Nancy's note: This is a variation on chocolate mousse that my mother has made on special occasions for as long as I can remember. It is so rich that it should be served in very small portions. When I was growing up, we had tiny French porcelain dessert crocks that we used only for this dessert, which made it seem even more special. At some point during my adulthood, my mother gave me the miniature crockery, so on the rare occasions that I want to make a dessert this rich, I can decorate my table with those same special dishes. You could just as easily serve it in small ramekins or even teacups.

Serves 6

6 ounces chocolate chips or other good-quality semi-sweet or dark
    chocolate, chopped
2 tablespoons sugar
1 dash salt
1 tablespoon vanilla
1 egg
¾ cup whole milk, heated to scalding but not quite boiling

Place chocolate, sugar, salt, vanilla and egg in food processor or blender and blend for 1 minute. Then, with blender or food processor running, slowly add the hot milk in a steady stream. Blend until well combined.

Divide among 6 cups. Chill 2-3 hours before serving.

Top with a small dollop of whipped cream, if desired.

Strawberry Meringue Torte

Nancy's note: This is another dessert for which people always request the recipe as soon as they taste it. It looks more complicated than it really is. For several years, I chaired the faculty appreciation luncheon at my children's elementary school, and my mother always contributed this dessert (even though grandparents weren't really expected to pitch in!). The teachers loved it. Note that it needs to sit for at least four hours, so start it in the morning for an evening event, or do it the day before.

Serves 8

5 egg whites, at room temperature
¼ teaspoon cream of tartar
1 cup sugar
1 teaspoon vanilla
2 cups heavy cream
¼ cup confectioner's sugar
2 teaspoons vanilla
3 cups sliced strawberries

Preheat oven to 275°F. Line two large cookie sheets with aluminum foil or parchment paper.

Draw three 7" circles on foil or parchment paper to use as guides.
In a large mixing bowl, beat egg whites until frothy. Add cream of tartar; beat on medium speed until soft peaks form.

Add sugar, a tablespoon or two at a time. Beat ½ minute between each addition; continue beating until stiff and glossy. On high speed, beat in 1 teaspoon vanilla.

Spread meringue evenly over the 7" circles you drew. Bake 1 hour or until very lightly browned. Remove from oven and let cool on cookie sheets on wire racks. Remove meringue rounds from sheets, wrap in plastic wrap, and set aside.

About four hours before serving, beat cream, confectioner's sugar, and vanilla in a large bowl at high speed until stiff peaks form. Put one meringue layer on a serving plate. Spread 1/3 of the whipped cream over the meringue and scatter 1/3 of the berries atop the whipped cream. Repeat with two more layers. Refrigerate for at least four hours. Slice with a serrated knife.

Triple Chocolate Peppermint Layer Cake

Nancy's note: This cake was on the cover of Bon Appetit *in December of 2001, and I have made it for Christmas Eve every year since. (In fact, when I asked my nieces, Sophie and Phoebe, what to include in this cookbook, they both said, "The Christmas Eve dessert.") My husband Rick's colleagues consider it a must-have at their holiday office potluck as well.*

Serves 10-12

Filling
8 ounces milk chocolate, finely chopped
½ cup whipping cream
1 tablespoon light corn syrup
½ teaspoon peppermint extract

Cake
1 cup flour
1/3 cup unsweetened cocoa
½ teaspoon salt
¼ teaspoon baking powder
¼ teaspoon baking soda
¾ cup unsalted butter, at room temperature
1 cup sugar
1/3 cup (packed) dark brown sugar
2 teaspoons vanilla extract
3 large eggs
½ cup buttermilk
1½ cups mini chocolate chips

Chocolate Glaze

8 ounces bittersweet (not unsweetened) or semi-sweet chocolate, finely chopped

½ cup butter, cut into pieces

1 tablespoon light corn syrup

¾ teaspoon peppermint extract

12 whole candy canes, coarsely chopped

To make filling

Place chocolate in medium bowl. Bring cream and corn syrup to simmer in small saucepan. Pour hot mixture over chocolate; add extract and let stand 1 minute. Whisk until mixture is smooth. Let filling stand at room temperature while cake is baking and cooling.

Next, make cake. Preheat oven to 350°F. Butter a 9-inch cake pan. Line bottom with parchment paper. Butter parchment.

To make cake

Whisk flour, cocoa, salt, baking soda, and baking powder in medium bowl to blend. Using electric mixer, beat butter in large bowl until light and fluffy. Gradually beat in both sugars, then vanilla.

Add eggs one at a time, beating well after each addition. Beat in dry ingredients alternately with buttermilk in two additions each. Mix in chocolate chips.

Transfer batter to prepared pan. Bake cake about 1 hour 5 minutes. Cool cake in pan on rack 5 minutes. Turn out cake onto rack. Peel off parchment. Cool completely.

To assemble

Using electric mixer, beat filling until fluffy, about 30 seconds. Cut cake horizontally in half. Spread filling over the cut side of one cake layer. Chill layer so that filling firms up a little, about 15 minutes. Then top with second layer, cut side down. Chill filled cake 20 minutes.

To make glaze

Stir chocolate, butter, and corn syrup in small saucepan over low heat until melted and smooth. Mix in extract. Cool glaze until just lukewarm but still pourable, stirring occasionally, about 20 minutes.

Pour glaze over center of cake, then spread quickly over top and sides. Sprinkle chopped candy canes over the top. Chill until glaze sets, about 1 hour.

To serve, slice with a very sharp knife.

INDEX

Almost Lasagna, 80

Apple Cake, 116

Apple Crisp, 117

Aunt Doris's Blueberry Cake, 118

Aunt Ruth's Broccoli Ring, 48

Baked Apricot Chicken, 68

Baked Fish with Mustard Sauce, 74

Banana Bread, Who's On First, 25

Bavarian Cabbage Soup, 36

Beet Spread, 2

Biscuits, Cream, 26

Blueberry Cake, Aunt Doris's, 118

Bread Pudding, Chocolate, 125

Bread, Herb, 31

Bread, Portuguese Sweet, 28

Bread, Pumpkin, 30

Bread, Who's On First Banana, 25

Brie en Croûte, 3

Broccoli Ring, Aunt Ruth's, 48

Brunch Enchiladas, 18

Cabbage Soup, Bavarian, 36

Cake, Apple, 116

Cake, Aunt Doris's Bluberry, 118

Cake, Chocolate Pistachio Marble, 124

Cake, Chocolate Zucchini, 119

Cake, Mud Pie, 128

Cake, Triple Chocolate Peppermint Layer, 133

Candied Curried Pecans, 6

Carolyn's Essential Salad Dressing, 47

Cauliflower, Roasted, 53

Cheddar Balls or Wafers, 4

Cheese, Egg and Ham Strata, 20

Cheesecake, Eggnog, 127

Cheesy Onion Cornbread, 27

Chèvre with Herbs and Olives, 5

Chicken Casserole, 69

Chicken Pasta Caesar Salad, 44

Chicken Stir-Fry, 71

Chocolate Bread Pudding, 125

Chocolate Crackles, 102

Chocolate Mousse Pie, 122

Chocolate Pistachio Marble Cake, 124

Chocolate Zucchini Cake, 119

Chowder, Turkey, 42

Cider, Hot Mulled, 16

Cider Pot Roast, 64

Cocoa Angel Pie, 126

Cold Curried Tomato Soup, 37

Cold Spinach Soup, 38

Cole Slaw, 45

Cole Slaw, Crunchy with Asian Flavors, 46

Corn, Veggie, and Grain Casserole, 85

Cornbread, Cheesy Onion, 27

Cottage Cheese Dip, 12

Cottage Cheese Pancakes, 32

Crab Cakes, 77

Cranberry Pie, Nantucket, 129

Cream Biscuits, 26

Creamy and Savory Mac & Cheese, 81

Crêpes, Swedish, 33

Crunchy Cole Slaw with Asian Flavors, 46

Crustless Quiche with Onions and Gruyère, 21

Cucumbers, Danish, 51

Curry Dip, 12

Danish Cucumbers, 51

Dates Stuffed with Almonds Wrapped in Bacon, 8

Didi's Potatoes, 59

Dip, Cottage Cheese, 12

Dip, Curry, 12

Dip, Peanut, 11

Dried Cherry Pilaf, 58

Easy Steak Marinades, 96

Eddie Elephant Cookies, 103

Eggnog Cheesecake, 127
Enchiladas, Brunch, 18
Enchiladas, Spinach 87
Fish, Baked with Mustard Sauce, 74
Fish Stew, Mediterranean, 75
Fresh Mint Sauce, 98
Fried Rice, 57
Frittata, Red Pepper and Red Onion, 23
Fudge Almond Torte, 120
Ginger Molasses Cookies, 104
Gnocchi, Skillet with Tomatoes, White Beans, and Greens, 83
Greek-Style Lamb Burgers, 66
Guacamole, 9
Hamburgers, Mill Iron Farm, 65
Herb Bread, 31
Hollandaise, Quick Sauce, 99
Holly Cookies, 108
Hot Chocolate, 14
Hot Mulled Cider, 16
Italian Roasted Vegetables, 54
Jocie's Mustard, 97
Judy's Lentil Soup, 39
Lamb Burgers, Greek-Style, 66
Lasagna, Almost, 80
Lentil Soup, Judy's, 39
Lentil Walnut Paté, 13
Mac and Cheese, Creamy and Savory, 81
Marinades, Easy Steak, 96
Mediterranean Fish Stew, 75
Meringue Cookies, 109
Meringue, Strawberry Torte, 131
Mexican Tortilla Casserole, Vegetarian, 88
Mill Iron Farm Hamburgers, 65
Mint Sauce, Fresh, 98
Mint Iced Tea, 15
Mud Pie Cake, 128
Mustard, Jocie's, 97
Nantucket Cranberry Pie, 129
Nuts, Candied Curried Pecans, 6
Nuts, Spiced Mixed, 7

Oatmeal Chocolate Chip Cookies, 105

Oatmeal, Slow-Cooked with Fruit and Nuts, 24

Omelet, Smoked Salmon and Caramelized Onion 22

Orange Rice, 56

Oven-Baked Rice, 55

Oyster Stew, 40

Pad Thai, 84

Pancakes, Cottage Cheese, 32

Pancakes, Potato, 60

Pasta with Cherry Tomatoes and Arugula, 82

Paté, Lentil Walnut, 10

Pat's Turkey Loaf, 73

Peanut Brittle, 110

Peanut Butter Chocolate Candies, 111

Peanut Butter Chocolate Chip Cookies, 106

Peanut Dip, 11

Pecans, Candied Curried, 6

Peppermint Layer Cake, Triple Chocolate, 133

Pie, Chocolate Mousse, 122

Pie, Cocoa Angel, 126

Pie, Nantucket Cranberry, 129

Pilaf, Dried Cherry, 58

Pineapple Barbecue Pulled Pork Sandwiches, 67

Pissaladière, 91

Poppycock, 114

Portuguese Sweet Bread, 28

Posole, Shrimp and Scallop, 76

Pot Roast, Cider, 64

Potato Pancakes, 60

Potatoes, Didi's, 59

Pots de Crème, 130

Pudding, Chocolate Bread, 125

Pudding, Yorkshire, 61

Pulled Pork Sandwiches, Pineapple Barbeque, 67

Pumpkin Bread, 30

Pumpkin Soup, Southwestern, 41

Quiche, Crustless, with Onions and Gruyère 21

Quick Hollandaise Sauce, 99

Red Pepper and Red Onion Frittata, 23
Reverse Chocolate Chip Cookies, 107
Rice, Fried, 57
Rice, Orange, 56
Rice, Oven-Baked, 55
Risotto, Vegetable, 86
Roasted Cauliflower, 53
Roasted Vegetables, Italian, 54
Roasted Winter Squash, 52
Salad, Chicken Pasta Caesar, 44
Salad, Tuna and Bulgur, 50
Salad Dressing, Carolyn's Essential, 47
Sauce, Fresh Mint, 98
Sauce, Quick Hollandaise, 99
Scallop, and Shrimp Posole, 76
Shrimp and Scallop Posole, 76
Skillet Gnocchi with Tomatoes, White Beans, and
     Greens, 83
Slow-Cooked Oatmeal with Fruit and Nuts, 24
Slow-Roasted Garlic and Lemon Chicken, 70
Smoked Salmon and Caramelized Onion Omelet, 22
Southwestern Pumpkin Soup, 41
Spiced Mixed Nuts, 7
Spinach and Cheese Pie, Greek (Spanakopita), 90
Spinach Enchiladas, 87
Spinach Soup, Cold, 38
Squash, Roasted Winter, 52
Steak Marinades, Easy, 96
Stew, Mediterranean Fish, 75
Stew, Oyster, 40
Stew, Thai Red Lentil, 92
Stew, West African Vegetable, 93
Stir-Fry, Chicken, 71
Strata, Cheese, Egg, and Ham, 20
Strawberry Meringue Torte, 131
Swedish Crêpes, 33
Tabbouleh, 49
Tea, Mint Iced, 15
Thai Red Lentil Stew, 92

Toffee, 112
Tomato Soup, Cold Curried, 37
Torte, Fudge Almond, 120
Torte, Strawberry Meringue, 131
Triple Chocolate Peppermint Layer Cake, 133
Truffles, 113
Tuna and Bulgur Salad, 50
Turkey Chowder, 42
Turkey Loaf, Pat's, 73
Vegetable Risotto, 86
Vegetables, Italian Roasted, 54
Vegetarian Mexican Tortilla Casserole, 88
West African Vegetable Stew, 93
Who's On First Banana Bread, 25
Yorkshire Pudding, 61
Zucchini Cake, Chocolate, 119

We hope you enjoy using the recipes in this book. Please contact us with comments, questions, suggestions, or any other feedback at www.nancyshohetwest.com/contact.

24418749R00087

Made in the USA
San Bernardino, CA
24 September 2015